Born in Lancashi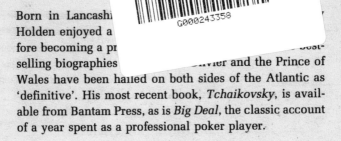 Holden enjoyed a fore becoming a pr selling biographies ....vier and the Prince of Wales have been hailed on both sides of the Atlantic as 'definitive'. His most recent book, *Tchaikovsky*, is available from Bantam Press, as is *Big Deal*, the classic account of a year spent as a professional poker player.

'A valuable sociological document, presented in most readable form. The blurb calls it "an important book". It is'
Peta Fordham, *The Times*

'Anthony Holden has collected and recounted the details of his [Young's] whole macabre story with the professionalism of a considerable reporter. His scrupulous presentation guarantees our total attention'
Leo Abse, *Spectator*

'Clear, detailed and vivid'
Charles Rycroft, *Times Literary Supplement*

'A well-documented and highly readable piece of journalism. A formidable account'
Evening News

'The utterly absorbing account, so disquieting as to be almost beyond belief, of the doings of Graham Young'
Dr Bernard Dixon, *New Scientist*

THE ST ALBANS POISONER

*The life and crimes of
Graham Young*

Anthony Holden

Now filmed as
*The Young Poisoner's
Handbook*

CORGI BOOKS

THE ST ALBANS POISONER
A CORGI BOOK : 0 552 14408 8

Originally published in Great Britain by
Hodder & Stoughton Ltd

PRINTING HISTORY
Hodder & Stoughton edition published 1974
Corgi edition published 1995

Set in 11pt Linotype Melior by Kestrel Data, Exeter.

Corgi Books are published by Transworld Publishers Ltd,
61–63 Uxbridge Road, London W5 5SA,
in Australia by Transworld Publishers (Australia) Pty Ltd,
15–25 Helles Avenue, Moorebank, NSW 2170,
and in New Zealand by Transworld Publishers (NZ) Ltd,
3 William Pickering Drive, Albany, Auckland.

Reproduced, printed and bound in Great Britain by
Cox & Wyman Ltd, Reading, Berks.

Contents

List of Illustrations

Key to Acknowledgements
[1] Hulton-Deutsch Collection
[2] Popperfoto
[3] Topix/The Scotsman Publications
[4] Mirror Syndication International
[5] The Press Association

THE ST ALBANS POISONER

*The life and crimes of
Graham Young*

1

A deep-going personality disorder

A psychopath, in layman's terms, is a person without moral sense, obsessively and at times aggressively so, who can yet appear perfectly civilized when it suits him. Whatever mental disturbance he has is elusive and equivocal, erupting spasmodically, after periods of calm, often in contrasting violence. He may well be highly intelligent, capable of making conventional moral judgements; yet his unpredictable and at times unseen mental lapses will submerge his sense of moral responsibility towards fellow human beings. Many of us may have been, at one time or another, on friendly terms with someone tinged, if not gripped, by psychopathy.

It is his powers of façade-building that make the psychopath more dangerous in a liberal than any other kind of society. He is conventional neither as a mental defective nor among the mentally disturbed. He is capable of social outrage, at worst murder, yet his veneer can protect him from becoming a social outlaw. The psychopath is at his most dangerous when he understands this, and understands it sufficiently to exploit the uncertainties of a liberal system.

Such a psychopath was the cold and calculating Graham Young. At every stage in what can only be called his career, he understood the system he was defying and turned its weaknesses to his own benefit. This is the story of a boy who, at the age of eleven, was more proficient than most men ever are in the use of chemicals and poisons. His frame of mind, whatever the influences that shaped it, was not unlike that of the pure scientist; the only difference, caused by his own personal brand of amorality, was that he contentedly chose human beings as his guinea pigs rather than guinea pigs. If the subject died, that proved no more than the success or failure of the experiment; the dosage and its effect went into his notebook and duly made him more expert. The most frightening aspect of his psychopathy is that those he was poisoning – his family, his friends, his workmates – thought him at best an innocent, at worst 'a little rum'.

Young's life falls into three distinct phases: his childhood, his years in Broadmoor, and his brief but active twelve months back in society before his final incarceration. But it is really two stories. The first is of a mind obsessed, of its development from harmless experimentation, which might have developed healthily, into an incarnate force for destruction, all the more appalling because its victims were so arbitrarily chosen. The second is of the world through which that mind moved, the people who tried to understand it, and of those who – with varying degrees of responsibility and resultant suffering – failed to.

Graham Frederick Young – Graham after a Scottish friend, Frederick after his father – was born in the maternity wing of Neasden Hospital, North London, on 7 September 1947. It was a difficult birth. His mother, Margaret, had developed pleurisy while pregnant, and Graham was born a 'blue baby'. He soon became perfectly healthy, but she – after a period of apparent recovery – was diagnosed as tubercular. An abscess was discovered at the base of her spine. Two days before the following Christmas, when Graham was barely three months old, she died.

Fred Young, a withdrawn and far from self-sufficient man at the best of times, broke down. Theirs had been a loving marriage, and Margaret – whom he'd called Molly – had been a devoted mother to their first child Winifred, then eight. Their daughter had been born in Aberdeen weeks before the outbreak of war, which brought the family south to Cricklewood. Fred, born a Londoner but brought up in Scotland by his widowed mother and an affectionate stepfather, worked as a charge-hand machine-setter for a clockmaking firm. There was nothing he could do but split his family up.

Luckily, close and loving relatives lived nearby. Winifred went to her grandmother in Links Road, while baby Graham was taken in by his Aunt Winnie, Fred's sister, who lived with her husband Jack Jouvenat at 768 North Circular Road. Fred stayed alone in their home at Dawpool Road for the time being, visiting the children each evening and at weekends. He would collect Winifred on the way round to Aunt Winnie's, then the two of them would push Graham's pram across the North Circular into the park surrounding the Welsh Harp reservoir.

Graham was an affectionate child, and soon developed a strong mother-son bond with his Aunt Winnie. He called the Jouvenats Auntie Panty and Daddy Jack, and became very dependent upon them, hating any separation. They in turn were delighted to see how well he got on with their own daughter Sandra, who although a few years older than Graham enjoyed playing with him when he was still only a toddler.

But in 1950, when Graham was still only two and a half, everything changed. Fred Young had met another Molly, this time an Irish one, who worked at the same firm and played the accordion at his local pub. The friendship grew to a loving mutual dependence, and on April Fool's Day 1950 they were married.

Fred, at thirty-three, was building himself a new life. By this time he had sold the Dawpool Road house, and was living with Winifred and her grandmother in Links Road.

Now he bought 768 North Circular Road from the Jouvenats, as a home for his children and their new stepmother. The Jouvenats moved to Links Road. So Graham, not yet three, stayed on in the home he had always known, but without the couple who had been parents to him. Instead there was a new woman to call Mummy, a woman his sister called Molly. And

14

the father and sister he had known as weekend visitors were suddenly around him all the time.

The change had no radical effect on him. But the tendencies he had always shown – quietness, shyness, a reluctance to join in any group activities – grew more marked. He began to read at an early age, and showed a precocious intelligence in his choice of books. His sister, also an avid reader, would take him to the local library, where he graduated from children's books to historical and military studies. The library was to play a big part in his childhood self-education, in itself the unconscious beginning of a sustained independence from any tuition but his own, and from any subjects but those he himself chose. It was to compensate for the irrelevance, and the uneasy competitiveness, of the classroom.

Young hated school. At the age of five he was sent to Braintcroft Junior School, Warren Road, where Winifred and Sandra were already popular older pupils. He was clearly a bright child, but he could never apply his intelligence to subjects which did not interest him. There were no science classes at Braintcroft, and history never seemed to reach the Twentieth Century. Although passable at English and history, he was a disaster at maths. He disliked being publicly shown inferior to other children when marks were totted up and reports paraded forth. So he took great delight in one extra-curricular activity at which he shone – acting. His triumph as an Ugly Sister in the Braintcroft Christmas pantomime is still remembered by his family and schoolfriends. It was the beginning of a lifelong

15

penchant for disguise and impersonation.

The Youngs' home life, meanwhile, had weathered its years of disruption and settled into a cosy, contented domesticity. The family say to this day that Graham got on well with his step-mother, Molly, and showed her great affection. But Young's own evidence, told to his schoolfriends as he grew older, is different. She was too strict, he said; she kept him short of clothes and pocket money. She would often lock him out of the house while Fred was at work, complaining to neighbours that Graham would eat the entire family food stock if left alone. She would leave him sitting alone outside the pub while she did her stint on the accordion. On one occasion, she smashed up all his model aeroplanes. Graham told friends that he hated her, and he later told a psychiatrist that he used to cry himself to sleep at nights, thinking of his real mother and wondering what life would have been like with her.

A close family friend at the time, Frank Walker, was convinced that Fred Young blamed Graham for his first wife's death. Mr Walker, whom Graham knew as Uncle Frank, noticed how much Fred Young had withdrawn into himself since Margaret's death. He was sometimes an unnecessarily brusque father to the mischievous Graham; their relationship always seemed strangely formal, never light-hearted, rarely showing overt affection on either side. Walker thought it a natural semi-conscious reaction for Fred to resent the child whose birth had accelerated his wife's death.

As he grew towards his teens, Young became increasingly solitary. His alert, inquiring mind found little to feed on in the modest, strait-laced home kept by Fred and Molly Young, and Graham spent more and more time at the library. When old enough to take books out, he sat for hours at the side of the Welsh Harp, absorbed in increasingly specialist texts – many of which he was careful not to take home. A plump child – his family called him 'Pudding' – he was always socially awkward, and never made friends easily in his family's company. He was nervous of strangers he met with them, especially friends of his sister and his cousin, only a few years older than himself. He would embarrass Winifred and Sandra by saying rude, outrageous or simply stupid things to friends they met casually, or by acts of deliberate naughtiness characteristic of a younger child – kicking over old ladies' shopping bags, teasing neighbours' pets. The only serious conversations he had were with older people he met when on his own in Gladstone Park; his family thought he was playing in the recreation ground, but usually found him talking earnestly to tramps and pensioners on park benches. Children his own age he shunned.

By the age of nine, the interests which were to shape Graham Young's life were clearly defined. His aunt and stepmother noticed that their scent and nail varnish bottles tended to disappear when nearly empty. They never understood why until one day Molly noticed a hole in Graham's school jacket, and found a half-empty bottle of acid in the pocket. She

17

also found him with a bottle of ether, which he told her he liked to sniff.

They now began to notice the kind of books he was bringing home. Studies of medical science, of crime, Black Magic, Nazism. Hitler seemed a particular obsession; Graham had found an old swastika badge, which he steadfastly refused to take off. He had grown more argumentative in the last year, and constantly upset his father by defending Nazi war policies. Family evenings became dominated by Graham's myopic harping on the war, and his oppressive, at times clandestine, pursuit of chemistry and medicine. For the first time, Graham's parents became worried about him. His interests, always a trifle bizarre, seemed to have become unhealthily obsessive. He had nothing at all in common with other children of his age in the area.

Molly decided something must be done. She questioned Graham closely about the acid and the ether in his possession, and he admitted looting the dustbins of a Neasden chemist's shop. Molly visited the chemist, to warn him what was going on; she also had a word with the librarian about Graham's taste in books. The chemist agreed to keep an eye out for him; the librarian reassured her that there was nothing abnormal about young boys taking an interest in war and militarism.

Black Magic was a little more frightening. Young told schoolfriends he had met a member of a Willesden coven – an unlikely-sounding tale, perhaps, but seemingly confirmed by his increasing expertise in the satanic arts. They coloured his early excursions into toxicology. Friends recoiled in horror when Graham urged them to join in ritual sacrifices of imaginary victims. Left to his own devices, he experimented with mice and, according to neighbours, local cats. Molly was truly shaken one day when going through his pockets, as was now her way, to find a wax model stuck with pins.

Clearly this was no ordinary child. But the family's failure to sense the demons at work within Graham – understandable when he was still so young and so close to them – was marked by an act of spontaneous generosity which in retrospect assumes heavy irony. Fred Young was keen for his son to follow his own career as an engineer, and was dismayed by his evident interest in, and aptitude for, more clinical forms of science. Graham himself plainly stated that engineering held no charms for him, and quoted his maths record as evidence of his inability. Fred maintained hopes that his son might change, and took pains to discourage his interest in science. Yet when Graham, rather to everyone's surprise, managed to scrape through his eleven-plus, his father's generous response was to present him with a chemistry set.

From Braintcroft, Young moved to the John Kelly Secondary (now Comprehensive) School in Tanfield Avenue, Willesden. Again, his performance in most subjects was mediocre, but his science master, Geoffrey Hughes, found his work impressive and placed him in the A stream. For the first time in his life, he made a couple of close friends outside

19

his own family – Clive Creager and Chris Williams, classmates who shared his interest in chemistry and liked to hear him air his knowledge. Young's class were all subjected to scientific lectures at one time or another, and so nicknamed him 'The Mad Professor'. He rather liked that.

Given a free hand in the chemistry laboratory, Young, Creager and Williams would experiment on mice. When the creatures had been dosed with bizarre concoctions, and studied closely as they died, Young would perform a post-mortem, taking his friends through all the orthodox procedures. Once he took a mouse home to perform a private autopsy in his bedroom; Molly was horrified and ordered him to throw it away. He vanished back to his room and drew a picture which he left lying downstairs when he went to school the next day. It showed the headstone of a tomb, with the inscription: 'In Hateful Memory of Molly Young. RIP.'

Drawing became another of Young's passions. Creager (who later became a dental student) sat next to him in class and recalls being passed drawings depicting them both. 'I would be hanging from some gallows over a vat of acid. Graham would be holding a flame to the rope. He liked drawing people on gallows with syringes marked "poison" sticking into them.' At home, Molly and Fred found drawings of coffins marked 'Mum' and 'Dad'.

Young's library reading had by now become more specific, and at the age of twelve he was more of an expert on toxicology than most laymen ever are. His chemical expertise was a help: already he could reel off the constituents of any medicine or pill around his home, and was eager to offer advice to family and friends with minor ailments. He would always call illnesses, even the common cold, by their long-winded medical names, and delighted in telling sufferers what could go wrong if they took an overdose of the most innocuous proprietary remedies.

He read any study of forensic medicine he could lay his hands on, and his memory for complex detail was phenomenal. Two books he read and re-read were *Sixty Famous Trials*, a standard compendium of famous cases told in slight detail, and – his special favourite – *Poisoner in the Dock* by John Rowland. Published in 1960, when Young was still twelve, the book's twelve chapters each deal with a different deadly poison, and a concluding chapter makes somewhat cursory efforts at distilling 'the mind of the poisoner'. Young loved the chapters on Palmer and Crippen, who joined Hitler in his gallery of heroes, but the section which most fascinated him at first was Chapter 2 – on antimony, or – as Young would insist on properly calling it – antimony potassium tartrate.

The chapter told the story of Dr Edward William Pritchard, the nineteenth-century Glasgow physician who poisoned his wife and her mother with antimony. It also mentioned the other famous antimony user, Charles Bravo, whose case remains unresolved. Much of the material in the chapter clearly gave Young ideas. From its seventeen pages he discovered that antimony was a slow-working poison, causing vomiting, cramp and intense stomach pain in the victim. The symptoms are often mistaken to indicate any variety of common illnesses, and death will result only if the poison is administered regularly over a sustained period. Young could have learned more from Pritchard's story; it was his vanity, his boasting, that finally gave him away. Like so many poisoners, Pritchard was skilful in his use of his materials, but sufficiently arrogant and self-obsessed to leave his tracks absurdly uncovered. He was executed in 1865, before an audience of 100,000 people.

Young never rated Pritchard very highly. He admired the man's dedication to his task, shared his relish in watching his victims die, but deplored his carelessness in failing to evade detection. For sheer notoriety, Crippen was his idol; for sheer villainy Dr William Palmer, who in all killed thirteen people with poison. Young openly boasted to Creager, Williams and other schoolfriends that one day his name would be as infamous as theirs. While they wanted to become engine drivers, dentists, salesmen, his one aim in life – to which he henceforth devoted himself single-mindedly – was to become a famous poisoner.

In April 1961, when he was thirteen and a half, Young went to Geoffrey Reis's chemist shop in Neasden High Street and asked for twenty-five grams of antimony. The minimum legal age for buying restricted poisons is seventeen, and Reis questioned the young boy closely. How old was he? Seventeen. What did he want the antimony for?

Young outlined a series of chemical experiments he had in mind, using his technical knowledge – and his acting ability – with good effect. Reis sold him the poison. 'I thought he looked rather small for his age,' said the chemist later, 'but I was convinced by his knowledge that he was older than he appeared.'

Fred Young gave his son two shillings and sixpence a week pocket money. Graham now took to mopping the floor at a local café for five shillings a week, and paid more visits to the chemist. Each time he signed the poison register in the name of M. E. Evans, giving a false address. He began to build up a stock of antimony, which he either carried around with him or kept in his school desk. He was never, however without a small phial of the poison, which he used to take out and show to his chums. He called it 'my little friend'. 'He would often get it out and pass it round,' Creager remembers. 'This is my little friend, he'd say, and chuckle over it like a gangster over his gun.'

The boys laughed when Young told them of his ambitions to be a famous poisoner. 'We treated it as a joke,' says Creager. 'It was the same with his admiration for Hitler. Graham would comb his short black hair over to one side, and hold the top of the comb to his upper lip. Then he'd strut about, repeating some Hitler speech in German. We all laughed. It was a good joke.'

But Young's behaviour was becoming a little too erratic for the other boys. He always tried to dominate any discussion, invariably seized any chance to assert his superior intelligence. Chris

Williams, who had always been a little closer than Creager to Young, started going around with another boy, Terry Hands. Young was upset. His pride was hurt, and he remembered the loneliness of his childhood. One day, after seeing Williams with Hands, he challenged Williams to a fight. Williams, the bigger of the two, won easily. 'I'll always remember that fight,' says Williams, now a car salesman. 'It was all over very quickly. Graham was much smaller than me. As he lay on the ground with me standing over him, he looked up and said to me: "I'll kill you for that".'

Williams, as usual, laughed. 'I didn't give it much thought. It's the sort of thing kids say when they've lost a fight. But some time afterwards – we'd patched it all up by then – Graham said to me: "You know, I really could kill you".'

A week later Chris Williams was taken mysteriously ill. He started vomiting violently during afternoon class, and had to go home. The day, he remembers, was a Monday; and the same thing happened again the following Monday. On each occasion, he realized later, he and Young had skipped school lunch together. Young had given Williams some sandwiches to persuade him to spend the lunch hour with him.

But Williams was not the brightest of children. He was ill at regular intervals for the next year, always after some sort of meeting with Young – yet he never suspected his strangely possessed schoolfriend of being responsible, for all his open talk about poisons and poisoners. Young took the chance to develop

24

one of his favourite tactics, which in later years he was to hone to a fine art: offering sympathy and medical advice.

In the spring of 1961, the two boys spent a Saturday together at the London Zoo. Young, as usual, provided the packed lunch. Williams was just recovering from a bout of his mysterious illness, and Young was eager to help. He'd brought along two bottles of lemonade – one, he said, specially treated with a powder to ease his friend's pains. Williams drank it gratefully, while Young consumed the other bottle. On his way home, Chris Williams was violently sick outside Finchley Road tube station, and spent the next few days in bed with dire stomach pains.

His symptoms were always the same: violent and copious vomiting, savage pains in his chest and stomach, fierce headaches, and occasional cramp in a number of limbs. He visited the family doctor, Dr Lancelot Wills, several times, but the GP could never find anything specifically wrong. Finally, he was taken to Willesden Hospital, where an intern diagnosed migraine. 'It got to the stage where we thought Chris was simply playing up,' said Mrs Williams. 'We were told we ought to take him to a psychiatrist.' They never did; and their son's bouts of illness continued. So did his close friendship with Graham Young.

It was while Young was poisoning Williams that his stepmother, Molly, found some antimony in his room at home. She didn't really know what it was, but the bottle was sufficiently clearly marked as a dangerous poison to raise the alarm. There was a monumental family row. Fred Young came the heavy hand, which he was not in the habit of doing, and forbade Graham to bring 'such things' into the house. Molly went round to speak to Geoffrey Reis, and told him not to sell any more poison to her stepson.

The following six months, the first half of 1961, were comparatively calm ones in the Young household. Graham's attentions seemed to turn to more natural scientific experiments for a child of his age. He started dabbling with fireworks, designing and making his own from cardboard and gunpowder. Conventional fireworks were not good enough for him; he would buy them in quantity, extract the gunpowder, and make what he liked to call his bombs. The family knew only slightly of this, as he used a hut in the Welsh Harp allotments as his laboratory. There was a narrow brush with the police one day when a Young prototype explosive half destroyed the hut, and poisons were found by officers inspecting the wreckage – but they were not traced to their source. Nor was it discovered at the time who blew up a neighbour's garden wall; the family later remembered they had chased Graham off that day, after finding him mauling their cat.

Graham was not a popular child in the neighbourhood. His bizarre interests and his eccentric behaviour made other parents keep their children away from him. He was often seen 'lurking', and would be pompously indignant when discovered and ticked off. When they learnt later what he had really been up to, people living around the North Circular Road blamed Young, probably with good reason, for a spate of deaths among the cats in the area, and began to wonder about every headache, every attack of collywobbles they themselves remembered having. Rumours naturally abounded, and still do, but there is no evidence that Young was responsible for any illnesses but those which began to beset his own family and Williams. The way his mind was working made it most unlikely that at this stage he poisoned anyone, apart from Williams, outside his own household. The only member to be spared was the one of whom he appeared most fond: Lemon, the budgie.

Since his stepmother's visit to Geoffrey Reis, Young – whose pocket money had now risen to four shillings a week – had been buying his poisons from another Neasden chemist, Edgar Davies, using exactly the same techniques – confounding the chemist's suspicions with a scientific lecture, and signing the register in the name of Evans.

Molly Young was ill twice in the early winter months of 1961. Each time she thought it was a bilious attack – the symptoms signified no more – and didn't bother much about it. Then Fred Young suffered a couple of similar attacks. Winifred, meanwhile, was deep in romance; she had met her future husband, Dennis Shannon, and spent a lot of her evenings – including her evening meals – at his family's home in Harlesden. One Spring evening in 1961, on her way to meet Dennis for an evening at the cinema, she too was violently sick. The family thought at first they must all have some kind of bug. They soon began to wonder if Graham had been using teacups or pots and pans for his chemical experiments, and had failed to wash them up properly; but Fred Young pointed out that he had forbidden Graham to conduct chemical experiments in the house. He didn't believe that the thirteen-year-old boy was defying him. Even if he were, it would all be rather a dreadful mistake – the kind of thing that life with Graham had accustomed them to. They never believed for one moment that the family baby could be deliberately poisoning them. The idea never arose. Graham indeed, was due some sympathy himself; one evening he went round to Aunt Winnie's after tea, and was sick all over her front doorstep.

Aunt Winnie, closer to Graham than any of them, was also the most astute member of the family. She realized early on that this was no ordinary sequence of illnesses; it must have some coherent, unorthodox explanation. Perhaps the water supply was contaminated. Perhaps there were rodents in the house. Perhaps the lead pipes were causing arsenic poisoning. She was the first to voice suspicions of Graham, but only to her husband Jack, who thought the whole idea preposterous. Nevertheless, she visited 768 North Circular Road less frequently, and made sure that Sandra never had so much as a cup of tea there.

Molly Young's attacks began to grow worse. She tried to keep the fact from Fred, as she didn't want

28

to worry him. She also quashed Winifred's suggestions and her own fears that Graham might be, at best indirectly, responsible; a sensitive woman, she was aware of Fred's feelings about his first wife's death, and didn't want to appear to be fomenting his feelings against Graham. Graham in turn was solicitous for Molly's welfare; he was always fetching her glasses of water, and even on occasion collecting her medicine from the chemist. Whether or not he was meanwhile doctoring the water or the medicine is not known; his own confession, confirmed by his subsequent practice, indicates that he was poisoning the family's food, their cups of tea and coffee, and occasionally slipping something into jars of sauce and chutney.

The household worries were not allayed by young Graham's further spates of macabre doodling. Never a great draughtsman, he confined himself to easily drawn insects and animals, such as spiders, snakes and birds of prey, while harping on the old themes of coffins, hanging men, poison bottles, syringes and skulls and crossbones. He left them lying all over the place, probably more through carelessness than design. The family, though increasingly disturbed, still put them down to Graham's unusual interests and youthful high spirits.

The summer passed, and the illnesses continued. Graham seems to have chosen his fourteenth birthday as the moment to step up his campaign. By his own word, it was in that September that poisoning his family became 'an obsession'. Molly's stomach pains became incessant. One morning in November,

Winifred noticed that her morning cup of tea tasted sour. She complained to Molly, who had made it; they thought it was perhaps a cup Winifred had used for mixing her shampoo, and threw it away.

On her way to work – she was now private secretary to a music publisher in Denmark Street – Winifred began to feel dizzy. Her eyes were out of control; the passengers on the tube seemed first to recede, then to lunge towards her. She was helped off the train at Tottenham Court Road, and managed to get to her office. But work was impossible. She could not focus her eyes on any writing. A workmate took her round to the Middlesex Hospital, where she spent the rest of the day undergoing tests. A bewildered doctor finally told her that she appeared to be suffering from belladonna poisoning.

Winifred got home in an angry mood. She openly accused Graham of being careless with his chemicals, and Fred Young conducted a searching domestic inquiry. Graham was sent to his room, where he spent the evening sobbing. In the end, she has recalled, Winifred felt such remorse that she apologized to him.[1]

Belladonna, traditionally the most romantic of poisons, is extracted from the plant deadly nightshade. It is so named from the Italian because it has been used in the preparation of women's cosmetics. Young bought it in the form of atropine from the Neasden chemist; by this time he had also supplemented his stock of antimony with arsenic,

[1]*Obsessive Poisoner*, Winifred Young, Robert Hale, 1973.

30

digitalis, tincture of aconite and – his ultimate favourite, deadliest and rarest of them all – thallium. While his family cast about for the causes of this persistent bug, fourteen-year-old Graham had hidden in his bedroom enough poison to kill 300 people.

Neighbours began to get worried about Molly. Still only thirty-eight, she had been a handsome woman when she married Fred Young twelve years before. The strain of living in the Young household had not really begun to tell until a few months before, when she suddenly started to look older. She constantly complained of stomach pains and back ache. They usually put it all down to an accident in the summer of 1961, when the bus she was travelling in crashed; Molly's seat overturned, throwing her upwards and cracking her head on the ceiling. But in the first few months of 1962 the change in her became dramatic; she grew thinner, more bowed. 'She seemed to be wasting away before our eyes,' recalled one friend. Molly once underwent hospital tests, but doctors could find no organic explanation for her symptoms.

On 21 April 1962, Easter Saturday, she woke up feeling dreadful. But this time the symptoms were different: she had a stiff neck, with pins and needles in her hands and feet. They would not go away. She decided to try and carry on as normal, however, and went out shopping. When she got home, she was feeling much worse. Fred was round at the pub having his lunchtime pint. Normally, he would take his son with him, and the two of them would sit on the bench outside, as Graham was still too young to be allowed in. Fred subsequently suspected him of taking the chance to dose his drink with poison while he nipped to the lavatory. On this Saturday, however, Graham said he wanted to stay at home. When Fred Young got back, he found his son staring through the kitchen window, watching Molly writhing in agony on the back lawn.

Fred insisted that she went to see Dr Wills, who could find no explanation and told him to take her to Willesden Hospital. When doctors, much to the family's dismay, insisted that she stay in for observation, Graham returned home on the bus to fetch her nightclothes. Molly remained light-hearted, joking with the nurses to keep her family's spirits up. In late afternoon, just after telling doctors she wanted to go home and get her husband's dinner, she died.

A post-mortem was considered essential, as Molly Young had died before doctors had even diagnosed what was wrong with her. The pathologist, Dr Donald Teare, attributed death to the prolapse of a bone at the top of her spinal column. But that still did not account for her condition. The most likely explanation still seemed to be that bus crash the previous summer. All those involved in Molly's death – family and medical staff alike – were so far from the truth that an inquest was not thought necessary.

Graham's contribution to easing the family's grief was to suggest that Molly should be cremated. It was much more satisfactory than burial, he argued, now that techniques of human incineration were so advanced. He harped on the theme with such persistence that Fred Young accepted the idea simply to shut him up.

Molly Young was cremated the following Thursday, 26 April. Graham was, of course, in the front row of the mourners at Golders Green crematorium. As he watched his stepmother's body slide into the flames, it seemed likely that at fourteen he had committed the perfect murder. It was not to be the last time that he thought he was watching the evidence of his crimes going up – with grotesque literalness – in smoke.

Young was never charged with Molly's murder. He was to be arrested within a month of her cremation, but police could not proceed against him when all the evidence had been destroyed. Soon afterwards, however, he told both police and his Aunt Winnie that he had been feeding antimony to his stepmother for more than a year – so long, in fact, and in such sustained non-fatal quantities that she had probably built up a resistance to the poison. It was when he realized this that, he claims, on 20 April, the night before she died, he doctored her evening meal with twenty grains of thallium – enough to kill a dozen people.

As the mourners gathered in the Youngs' front room after Molly's funeral, young Graham was the object of most sympathy. A neighbour remembers seeing him peering through the lace curtains that morning, and feeling intensely sorry for a boy deprived of his second, in some ways his third, mother – and still only fourteen. The boy himself

33

appeared genuinely moved by his stepmother's death. Its suddenness and her comparative youth leant an exceptionally heavy atmosphere to the proceedings. It was in some ways a welcome diversion when Molly's brother-in-law, Graham's Uncle John, began to vomit violently after eating a ham sandwich.

Uncle John was the only guest to have helped himself to some mustard pickles provided with the sandwiches. Antimony was an unbidden guest even at the wake. But to Graham this was little more than a passing practical joke. He decided now to turn his attentions to the victim logically next in line – his father Fred. What more natural that Fred Young should die within weeks of his second wife – killed by a broken heart?

Molly's death plunged Fred Young back into the deep despondency he had known twelve years before. The day after her funeral, he sat his children down and asked for their help in keeping the home going. He told them he had just managed, after ten years of careful economy, to pay off the mortgage on 768 North Circular Road. He had intended it as security for Molly's future, expecting that he would be the first to die. Now it would pass to Winifred and Graham. In retrospect, Fred thought that little chat might have sealed his fate.

His worst illness so far had been during Molly's first brief, fruitless stay in hospital for observation. It was the school holidays, and Fred – who always came home for lunch, preferring Molly's cooking to his works canteen – was in charge of the midday meal for himself and Graham. Winifred would cook them something decent at night, so Fred – never much of a chef – would just open a couple of cans at lunchtime. On this occasion he and Graham had corned beef and tinned pineapple. An hour after getting back to work, he felt so ill he thought he was going to die. The stomach pains and vomiting were worse than he had ever known them. But, like Molly, Fred was always reluctant to rush straight off to a doctor, so he decided to sit it out. By evening he was feeling himself again.

Fred was shaken by the severity of the attack. But he seemed to recover quickly enough, and soon put it behind him. Then the pains, the vomiting and the diarrhoea all started again and – though less violent – did not let up. The attacks always seemed to come on a Monday, and the pain would gradually ease off over the rest of the week. During this period, Fred later realized, it was on Sunday evenings that Graham accompanied him to the pub.

During Molly's last weeks, Fred Young was spared further illness. But only days after her death he suffered another really serious attack. Winifred had again spent the evening with the Shannons, and Fred had eaten with Graham. All the old symptoms – stomach pains, vomiting, diarrhoea – returned and this time they persisted in earnest. Fred stuck it for a few days, then at Winifred's behest went to Dr Wills. Again the GP could find no specific cause for the illness, and could only suggest hospital. Fred was just pooh-poohing the idea when he collapsed on the surgery floor. An ambulance was called, and

Fred found himself in Willesden General Hospital, where his wife had died less than two weeks before.

Graham, of course, came to visit him, but Fred always felt uneasy in his presence. Graham would sit by the bedside staring at his father, saying little, but seizing any chance to discuss Fred's condition with medical staff. Finally, something in Fred Young seemed to snap. When Frank Walker took Graham to see him one day, he said: 'Get that boy away from me.'

Fred made a partial recovery, and came home. But he was worse again within a couple of days, and the two Winifreds insisted on calling an ambulance to take him back. When they all went to visit him that evening, doctors told them with some astonishment that the latest preliminary tests seemed to indicate either arsenic or antimony poisoning. The family were horrified; all of them instinctively looked at Graham. But he was absorbed in explaining to the doctors how they could distinguish between the two poisons.

Antimony poisoning was confirmed the next day. Fred Young was told that one more dose would have killed him. As it was, he had a good chance of recovery, but his liver would be permanently damaged. When Aunt Winnie visited her brother that evening, he asked her to look after Graham – and to keep him away from the hospital.

At home, Graham remained remarkably calm while the rest of the family were both anxious about Fred and disturbed by their private suspicions. Aunt Winnie decided to confront Graham – against her husband's wishes – and asked him directly if he had poisoned his father. Graham flatly denied it, appearing very hurt that she could even imagine such a thing.

At school, he told his friends that his father was now ill and in hospital – just a fortnight after his stepmother's death. Clive Creager was convinced Graham had poisoned his family, and told his parents so. But the Creagers decided against going to the police, having no evidence at all on which to lay such a grave charge against so young a boy.

While all those around Young dithered, refusing to believe what they increasingly feared, it was his science master who decided to act. Having encouraged Graham to make full use of the laboratory, he had become alarmed at the kind of experiments the boy was conducting. He would never adopt suggestions for conventional chemistry exercises. Instead, he would bring in any number of different poisons and spend hours analysing, meticulously recording his conclusions in a notebook.

Mr Hughes decided one night to take a look at that notebook, which Young had never volunteered to show him. He stayed late at the school, and went through Graham's desk. In it he found, not to his surprise, several bottles of poison. In the notebook he found drawings of dying men, poetic odes to different poisons and poisoners, and illustrated essays about Palmer and Crippen. Recalling Chris Williams's recurring and still unexplained illness, he decided to take his suspicions to the headmaster, who immediately admitted that he too had been concerned about Young's evident eccentricity.

Together, the two men visited Dr Wills, who told them of the illnesses in the family throughout the past year. But it would still be premature, they concluded, to go to the police. Instead, they arranged for a psychiatrist to speak to Young in the guise of a careers officer from the Child Guidance Service.

Graham gave his family a full and enthusiastic account of the meeting. He had been told, above all, that he was bright enough to aim for a university place. His chemistry was outstanding, but he would have to brush up his maths. Evidently, Young had been seduced into a long monologue on his obsession with poisons, his knowledge of toxicology and the controlled experiments he had been conducting in the labs. In a pattern of events which was to repeat itself with uncanny accuracy ten years later, he had allowed his own vanity to betray him. Young thought he had given a dazzling display, that the welfare officer had been much impressed, and that a bright career lay ahead of him. What he didn't know was that the psychiatrist had gone straight to the police.

Detective Inspector Edward Crabbe called at the family home next day, 21 May. In Graham's room he found three books – *A Handbook on Poisons, Sixty Famous Trials* and *Poisoner in the Dock*. He also found varying quantities of antimony, thallium, digitalis, ionine, atropine and barium chloride. He went round to Links Road to await Young's return from school, telling his unsurprised but distraught aunt that her nephew would be arrested for the malicious administration of poison.

Young walked calmly past the waiting police car and straight through the front door. He was stinking of ether, but explained to his aunt that he'd been sucking Victory V Lozenges. He greeted the police with complete self-confidence. Told to turn out his pockets, he piled the table high with nothing but the usual schoolboy rubbish. He was then told to remove his shoes and socks, which again produced nothing untoward. But when he took off his shirt, out fell his 'little friend' – his phial of antimony – and two small, full bottles. He bluntly told the Inspector he didn't know what they contained. They were taken off for analysis, which proved the substance to be thallium. Young was removed to Harlesden police station.

All that night, under close questioning, he denied everything. When Aunt Winnie and his sister came down after taking the news to Fred in hospital, he refused to speak to them. They told the police, however, about the belladonna in Winifred's tea, and he was accused of poisoning her. Next morning he made a full confession, and revealed various other hiding-places, including a hedge near his home, where police subsequently found caches of poison. At magistrates court that day he was charged with poisoning Chris Williams, Fred Young and Winifred Young, and remanded for trial at the Old Bailey.

The family were filled more with horror than

remorse. They still rejected suggestions that Young's activities must have been obvious for some time. Fred said that only when police came to question him in his hospital bed, where he was still lying close to death, did things really 'fall into place'. All Graham's family, especially Auntie Winnie, had had increasing suspicions; but they maintained that it was impossible to believe a thirteen-year-old boy had been poisoning his own closest relations. They were even frightened by the idea, clearly a more sympathetic one, that he had been accidentally contaminating the crockery or the food.

Apart from natural family instinct, the deception can also be accounted for by Young's emergent psychopathy. Psychiatric examination in Ashford remand centre showed that he was quite capable of concealing all malevolence, if indeed he felt any. The clinical verdict was 'lack of moral sense'. Young's choice of victims, in both his murderous phases, must be explained by complete amorality. It is possible to cite various trivial incidents that could have provoked feelings of hostility towards each of them, just as it is to argue that his lack of a real mother in the first years of his life, and the constant changes of proxy mother, lay behind his abnormality. But throughout his campaigns the common characteristic he showed was the detached objectivity of the self-educating scientist.

He chose the victims closest to hand primarily because he could observe and note the results of his experiments — not so much with the poisoner's traditional callousness as with the scientist's precision of method. The only remark he ever made which colours this slightly, came during this spell in Ashford remand centre: 'I miss my antimony,' he told a psychiatrist who had noticed he looked downcast. 'I miss the power it gives me.'

Young appeared at the Old Bailey, before Mr Justice Melford Stevenson, on 6 July 1962. He was fourteen years and nine months old.

He spoke only once during the trial, when he pleaded guilty to all three counts. Mr E. J. P. Cussens, prosecuting, said it was clear Young had a great knowledge of poisons, and that he seemed to take 'a strange and dangerous interest' in them. It was apparent that for some considerable time the boy had been buying at chemists' shops poisons dangerous enough to be on the poisons register.

After outling the illnesses suffered by Williams, Fred and Winifred, counsel read the statement made by Young at Harlesden police station:

'I have been interested in poisons, their properties and effects since I was about eleven. I tried out one of them on my friend Williams. I gave him two or three grains at school. I cannot remember how I caused him to take it. I think it was probably on a cream biscuit or a cake. He was sick after taking it. Later I gave him other doses, always on food.

'After that I started experimenting at home by putting sometimes one and sometimes three grains of poison on prepared foods which my mother, father and sister would eat. I must have eaten some of the poisons myself occasionally because I became sick as well.

'After eating the food, all my family were sick. By September of last year this had become an obsession with me and I continued to give my family small doses of antimony tartrate on prepared foods. One morning at the end of November I was getting ready to go to school when I saw my sister's cup of tea on the dresser. I put one-tenth of a grain of belladonna in the milk, and left for school. That night my mother told me my sister had been ill during the day. She told me what the symptoms were and I knew it was the effect of the belladonna. I gave some of the remainder to Williams.

'On occasions I have also put antimony tartrate solution and powder on foods at home which my mother and father have taken. My mother lost weight all the time through it and I stopped giving it to her about February of this year. After my mother died on 21 April this year I started putting poisons at home in milk and water and on food. As a result my father became ill and was taken to hospital. I then realized how ill he was. I cannot think of anyone else I have given poison to.

'I knew that the doses I was giving were not fatal, but I knew I was doing wrong. It grew on me like a drug habit, except it was not me who was taking the drugs. I realize how stupid I have been with these poisons. I knew this all along, but I could not stop it.'

Mr Cussens then said that poisoning had nothing to do with Molly Young's death. A post-mortem had proved that it was due to natural causes. But Dr Donald Blair, a consultant psychiatrist who

42

examined Young at Ashford, said in his report: 'He gave his mother so much antimony that I can't help wondering whether it could have been in any way responsible for the condition of her vertebral column which led to her death.' No-one knew at that stage about the thallium administered the night before she died.

Next to give evidence was Dr Christopher Fysh, senior medical officer at the Ashford remand centre, who said that in his opinion Young was suffering from a psychopathic disorder. He was not suffering from any mental illness. 'In my opinion he requires care in a maximum security hospital, and there is accommodation for him at Broadmoor.'

Then followed an exchange between Dr Fysh and Mr Justice Melford Stevenson which was to become justly famous ten years on.

Judge: 'The boy uses the word "obsession". What do you think about that?'

Fysh: 'Poisons have tended to take an extremely prominent place in his mind because of the sense of power they gave him . . . He considers himself very knowledgeable about the effects of poisons.'

'Can you express a view as to the prognosis?'

'I feel it is bad.'

'Does that mean that this behaviour is likely to be repeated if the opportunity were available?'

'I think it is extremely likely.'

Miss Jean Southworth, for the defence, asked Dr Fysh: 'Do you accept that he knew what a fatal dose was?'

'In some cases, yes. But in others, no.'

'Do you agree he has not the killer instinct?'

'I would say he is rather prepared to take the risk of killing.'

'Is it not possible that normal treatment in a hospital rather less forbidding than Broadmoor might be equally suitable?'

'At the request of the Ministry of Health, the boy was examined by Dr James Cameron of the Maudsley Hospital. Dr Cameron came to the conclusion that he was far too dangerous to be in even that hospital.'

Dr Blair's report was then presented. It began:

'He is obviously highly intelligent, but his emotional responses are slow and he has never exhibited the slightest distress in relating the instances of poisoning.

'Indeed, he seemed to experience emotional satisfaction in doing so, and particularly in revealing his intimate knowledge of the toxicology of the various drugs concerned. His attitude to the whole matter was unrealistic, and he did not seem to be able to appreciate that he had indulged in acts for which he deserved any serious reprehension.

'He told me of his great interest in drugs and their poisonous effects, but was unable to reveal any reason for such interest. He said he had no grievances against any of his relatives or his friend, and indeed thought he loved them quite well. It just seemed that they were the nearest people to hand for his purpose.'

Dr Blair's conclusion, like that of Dr Fysh, was to have a macabre echo ten years later:

'There is no doubt in my mind that this youth is at present a very serious danger to other people. His intense obsession and almost exclusive interest in drugs and their poisoning effect is not likely to change, and he could well repeat his cool, calm, calculating administration of these poisons at any time.'

In response to a criticism from Miss Southworth, the judge ordered an inquiry into the circumstances in which Young obtained his poisons. He then extracted from her the agreement that in view of the medical evidence, which was uncontradicted, there was 'no practical alternative' to Broadmoor.

Under Section 66 of the 1959 Mental Health Act Mr Justice Melford Stevenson then committed Young to Broadmoor, adding a restriction order that he must not be released without the express authority of the Home Secretary for a period of fifteen years.

2

An extremely full recovery

Broadmoor Hospital was opened in 1863 at Crow-thorne in Berkshire, thirty miles from London, as an asylum for criminal lunatics. As terminology has changed with the times, so Broadmoor is now classed, with Rampton and Moss Side, as one of three 'special hospitals' in England dealing with mentally ill offenders, or mentally handicapped people with violent or criminal tendencies. Its independence from the prison system is as jealously prized as its separate identity: in 1948 control passed from the Home Office to the Department of Health, although the Home Secretary retains supervision of most admissions and releases. And in recent years newspapers have frequently been criticized by the Press Council for referring to Broadmoor's inmates as 'criminals' rather than 'patients'.

The courts remain the major stepping-stone to Broadmoor; about sixty-five per cent of the hospital's population at any one time have been sent there after conviction. But some twenty-five per cent have never been convicted of any crime, having been charged but found unfit to plead; the remaining ten per cent may never have had any conflict with the law, being sent to Broadmoor from conventional psychiatric or mental hospitals for displaying violent tendencies.

But Broadmoor's frequently heightened redbrick Victorian walls remain as gaunt and forbidding as they were a hundred years ago, and conditions inside – which have received as little structural alteration – are made much worse by gross overcrowding. Designed to accommodate 450 patients, the hospital eventually housed more than 750. In evidence to the Parliamentary Estimates Committee's 1968 inquiry, a senior charge nurse said: 'We really do not do much more for the patients than a farmer would for his animals. We are attending to their basic bodily needs; we are maintaining observation and discipline, but we are certainly not doing the job that the hospital should be doing.'

The Committee themselves were 'appalled to see the extent of the overcrowding in the century-old Broadmoor building'. A Health Ministry witness said in evidence: 'We were all shocked when we first saw Broadmoor . . . By present day standards the hospital is not adequate for more than 500 male patients . . . As a result, there is in Broadmoor a day room with thirty-five beds crowded into it, a medical ward which patients have to use as an overflow dining-room, a corridor used for the same purpose, and seven beds placed in a corridor. Staff rooms have had to be turned into accommodation for patients.' These problems, however, cast no adverse reflection on the staff, 'the value of whose work in such conditions is even greater than it would otherwise be'. Mrs Renée Short, Labour MP for Wolverhampton North East, who headed the inquiry, summed up on presenting her report to the public: 'Conditions were frightful.'

Overcrowding, Broadmoor's dominant problem, has not eased since 1968. Another Estimates Committee member, Mr Edward Rowlands, then Labour MP for Cardiff North (now for Merthyr Tydfil) said prophetically: 'Even if a firm decision is taken now to build a new special hospital, the pressure cannot begin to ease for another five years.' A firm decision was taken – to build a fourth special hospital at Park Lane, Liverpool, adjacent to Moss Side – but building work was twice delayed by Government cutbacks in spending. The inter-departmental battles which dogged its planning made clear the priorities forced on special hospitals by the residents of areas in which they are built: Park Lane has been designed not by Department of Health architects, even though they were responsible for the revamping of Holloway Prison, but by Environment Department architects, specialists in high security institutions. The corollary to Broadmoor's overcrowding is stark in its simplicity: staff have time to do no more than maintain security. Obviously this is a high priority in an institution one-third of whose population are convicted murderers, but it has traditionally been at the expense of therapeutic treatment. In the early 1970s there were a mere eight psychiatrists at Broadmoor, with full-time medical responsibility for between

750 and 800 patients, many of whom are shrewd enough to realize that an escape attempt is taken as indication of willingness to return to the world outside, and so as a criterion of mental recovery. Department of Health architects were allowed to modify the Park Lane plans, but further internecine strife delayed the project even more. (For current conditions in the 'special hospitals', see the epilogue.)

Escapes from Broadmoor are comparatively rare – an average of one every other year since 1920 – but each naturally provokes national outcry. The two public inquiries into Broadmoor since the last war have been prompted by escapes – the first, in 1962, by the most infamous event in Broadmoor's history before Graham Young's release. John Thomas Straffen was committed there in 1951, after being found unfit to plead on charges of murdering two small girls, aged six and nine. In the six months before his escape from Broadmoor, he was said to be a 'model patient'; under his regulation clothing, meanwhile, he wore a pin-stripe suit. In April 1962 he got over the wall; his liberty was only brief – the suspicions of a warder's wife led to the alarm being raised – but long enough for him to strangle a five-year-old girl, Linda Bowyer, as she picked bluebells in a nearby Berkshire wood. An inquiry was set up under Mr J. Scott Henderson QC into security arrangements in Broadmoor; its only tangible outcome was a siren system on the hospital walls to warn local residents of an escape (in spite of evidence that the first thing escapees did was to get as far away from Crowthorne as possible).

The siren was not sounded in July 1958, when the notorious Frank Mitchell escaped by cutting through iron bars with a hacksaw; hospital authorities were satisfied he was out of the area before they learned he had gone. Mitchell, a highly dangerous aggressive psychopath, had already escaped once from Rampton, for which he was sentenced by Mr Justice Finemore – with a comment that he should never have been sent to Rampton in the first place – to nine years in an orthodox state prison. Mitchell claims to have 'swung the lead' in prison by pretending to be a mental defective, so that he could win a transfer to Broadmoor. A report made after his escape from Broadmoor, where he had been transferred on precisely those grounds, revealed that he had been birched twice during his imprisonment, on the grounds that 'there was no evidence' of mental instability to explain his violent behaviour.

The inquiry into all three special hospitals set up in the aftermath of Mitchell's escape reported to the Health Minister, Mr Enoch Powell, in April 1961. It concluded that a patient 'should be accepted for admission to one of the special hospitals only after all other possibilities have been examined and found unsuitable'. This was because 'it is wrong to place unnecessary restrictions on the individual, because it is expensive and wasteful in terms of staff and money to provide elaborate precautions for patients who do not really need them, and because it is more difficult for a patient to be absorbed into the community if it is known that he has been in a special hospital'. The

51

report recommended that 'as far as possible, patients should be treated locally. Security arrangements short of those provided at special hospitals should be provided in the National Health Service, and psychiatric services should be arranged to ensure a variety of types of hospital units and to enable transfers to be made between them. For patients who present special difficulty, because of aggressive, anti-social or criminal tendencies, diagnostic and treatment centres should be set up. These would provide an investigatory and diagnostic service for patients, provide treatment, and also provide facilities for research. Close liaison should be maintained between these and the remand and observation centres being set up under the penal system.'

Mr Powell accepted the report's major recommendations. The new remand centre system seemed, however, to work more effectively in ensuing years than the local NHS screening process, and became the focal point of most diagnostic and recommendation work. The residents of Crowthorne, to be sure, were not in the least reassured, and in 1964 successfully pressed for a reduction in their rates – ten per cent for those living within a mile of the hospital, five per cent for those between one and two miles away. Continuing unease in 1966 moved their MP, Mr William van Straubenzee, to urge that Broadmoor be the subject of further inquiry – as part of Lord Mountbatten's commission into prison security. His request was refused, although it had timely support in the form of three rooftop protests by Broadmoor inmates during the previous month.

It was hospital staff who set the pace in Broadmoor protests after Mr van Straubenzee's vain attempt. They consistently contacted newspapers with alarming stories of violence, attempted escapes, attacks on nurses, more rooftop sieges and drug-smuggling (during the famous purple hearts scare) within the hospital. In 1967 they went so far as to commission their own report on the hospital, under the auspices of the Prison Officers Association. Only twelve of the 168 nurses who gave evidence said they were satisfied with existing security arrangements. Morale of nursing staff was said to be 'at an almost disastrously low level', largely because of the massive overtime necessary to maintain discipline, which had 'steadily declined over the years because there is no obvious lead to staff and patients'.

The report was used as a basis for repeated pay claims by Broadmoor staff, who periodically worked to rule on this issue after the 1967 evidence. But more significantly, this report was the first to suggest a trend of great relevance to the case of Graham Young, who had by now been in the hospital five years. 'Gross indiscipline and violence,' it said, 'have produced rapid discharges from Broadmoor, a premature move to better conditions in Broadmoor, or a return to prison.' Broadmoor, it continued, 'fails in its role when it returns patients to prison simply because they are too violent to handle.' Then, crucially, it added: 'Broadmoor is guilty of callous disregard for public safety when it discharges patients for the same reasons.'

*　　*　　*

It was against this developing background that Graham Young entered Broadmoor in July 1962. He was not, as has been said, the youngest person ever to go there. Only three months before Young's arrival, an eighty-seven-year-old patient named Bill Giles had died there after spending seventy-seven years within the hospital walls. Giles had been committed to Broadmoor in 1885, at the age of ten, for setting fire to a hayrick. Because of his age he had spent his first five years in the female wing. As the years went by, he had become a favourite patient, and was given an official present by the authorities each year on his birthday; the Broadmoor tailor was sent along to Block Four to measure him for a new grey suit.

But Young was one of only three boys under sixteen to be sent there this century. Conditions in the admission block, with the enforced company of offenders, many of them violent, in varying stages of as yet untreated mental illness, could only be traumatic to one scarcely adolescent. They are bad enough for older men whose abnormalities are only slight and temporary. One such was Peter Thompson, the campaigner for penal reform and, joint chairman with Lord Longford of the Thompson-Pakenham Committee, who arrived in Broadmoor's admission block as a bewildered patient (he thought he'd been sent to Dartmoor) in 1965. In his autobiographical essay, *Bound for*

Broadmoor[1], Thompson has graphically described what confronted him:

'One patient made a habit of washing himself in his own urine and then using a communal towel to dry himself. The permanent overcrowding and shortage of staff makes this even worse. At nights, twenty patients share one commode to a dormitory. On the two or three occasions a year when "Berkshire Belly" strikes – an outbreak of diarrhoea and vomiting – the situation can be degrading. I remember a night when thirteen men were queueing to use the commode. By the time the last one used it, the thing was overflowing and the stench was appalling; and it was not even possible to open a window, for security reasons, nor wash one's hands. This kind of situation strips away one's last vestige of human dignity.'

Young was given a private room in the reception block, where he was to spend his first six months. It had a studded green door, a small barred window with two-inch thick wooden shutters, and the luxury of a rug on the floor. The bed was screwed down. Like all other newcomers – among them a schizophrenic who had axed his wife to death – Young was roused each morning at seven a.m., and allowed to read, play billiards, watch television and make rugs until lights-out at eight p.m. Certain times of day were set aside for outdoor exercise in the 'airing courts'.

[1]*Bound for Broadmoor*, Peter Thompson (Hodder and Stoughton, 1972).

As throughout his life, the boy did not make friends easily. His tendency to keep apart, and to be arrogant and stand-offish when others tried to befriend him, made him unpopular. Nurses kept a special watch to ensure there was no bullying or victimization, and were especially vigilant against the attentions of homosexuals. Former Broadmoor patients all testify that homosexuality is widely and openly practised in the hospital, where the minority of women patients are strictly segregated. But there is no evidence that Young was in any way abused by or involved with homosexuals during his nine years there.

He was probably protected as much by his asexuality as anything else. Psychiatrists have searched for a sexual element in Young's psychopathy, but he has never demonstrated anything more than a mild misogyny. He and Chris Williams had had a playful relationship with a girl called Jean, who worked at the library. On one occasion, Williams believes, Young dosed his friend, ensuring a twenty-four-hour sickness, so there could be no squabble about who took Jean to a Dickie Henderson TV show recording at Wembley. But she was the only flirtation in Young's life, and that at the age of twelve.

The first Broadmoor visits by Young's family – he was officially allowed a total of seven a month, though he never received anything like that – were dismal affairs. Fred Young, whose visits were soon to cease altogether, sat totally silent. Graham would at first be quiet and unresponsive, then would warm to telling his family about the gory deeds behind other inmates' incarceration. Soon, however, Fred Young sold up the North Circular Road house, and moved with Jack and Winnie Jouvenat to a new home in Sheerness, Kent, so Graham was to see less of them. Fred could rarely be persuaded to make the trip to Berkshire, still brooding as he was about what his son had done to him and his wife. Aunt Winifred remained among the faithful regulars, as did Winifred, by now married to Dennis Shannon and living in Hemel Hempstead, Hertfordshire, with their first child on the way.

Other family friends, like Uncle Frank Walker, would also visit Graham occasionally. Mr Walker remembers Young requesting endless boxes of matches; he took them along, thinking it an innocent enough request, worried only slightly about the smoking habits of one so young, until someone told him about the poisonous properties of phosphorus.

The first problem confronting the Broadmoor authorities was Young's education. Consultations were held with the Berkshire education authority, whose director of special services, Mr Dudley Fiske, was commissioned to find a private tutor for the boy. Psychiatric evidence had shown his IQ to be well above average – a not unfamiliar phenomenon among Broadmoor patients – and suggested that sustained education towards GCE O and A levels might make a fruitful supplement to other methods of treatment. But there is no legal requirement for the state to provide education to those detained for breaking the law.

A Welshman named Williams already conducted some classes in English, history and languages at the hospital, but they were irregular and always poorly attended. It was also thought that Young might benefit from the special relationship a personal tutor would provide. A shortage of part-time teachers, however, and a reluctance on the part of those approached to take the job on, made finding Graham a mentor unexpectedly difficult. Discussions went as high as the Minister, Mr Powell. But just as one had been found, Young announced that he had no wish for private lessons; and his rejection of Berkshire's offer was supported, rather to the education officer's surprise, by Broadmoor psychiatrists. They believed that Young could and would use the hospital library and the visiting mobile library to pursue the subjects that interested him. They were to be proved quite right.

The worst fears of Young's medical overlords and fellow inmates seemed to be confirmed less than a month after his arrival, by a sudden death in one of the outlying blocks. John Berridge, a twenty-three-year-old former soldier who had been sent to Broadmoor after shooting both his parents, collapsed with convulsions and quickly died in ward three of block four on the night of 6 August 1962. Post-mortem examination showed that death was due to cyanide poisoning.

The immediately held inquiry established that no cyanide was at the time kept at Broadmoor, either in its natural form or in any by-product from which it could be easily extracted. The investigation centred on means by which the poison could have been smuggled in, either by visitors or by post, until it was pointed out that the farmland adjacent to Broadmoor's boundaries was thick with laurel bushes – from which an expert poisoner could extract sufficient cyanide to kill the entire hospital population several times over.

Not surprisingly in such an institution, there were any number of suspects offering candid confessions, and among them was Graham Young. Chief suspect in the eyes of other patients, he made great currency out of explaining in meticulous detail the processes for extracting cyanide from laurel leaves. But the authorities remained unconvinced, and the most widely held unofficial explanation was suicide. The source of the cyanide was never unequivocally discovered, and the case has always remained open.

Nonetheless, Young was henceforth regarded by the hospital population with unremitting suspicion. He enjoyed this, of course, and compounded their fears by developing his old skill in talking like a medical textbook. Plans for transferring him to a longer-term block with better conditions were changed, and he was kept in room five of the admission block's Ward One indefinitely. With a long stay in prospect, he began to decorate his room with pictures of Nazi leaders and other polemic emblems. He painted skulls and crossbones on the containers provided for his tea, sugar and so on, changing the names on their labels to those of polysyllabic poisons. He read William Shirer's *The Rise and Fall of the Third Reich* continuously over several years, and combined his further study of medical and toxicological textbooks – to which he had unrestricted access at both libraries – with a reading of Bram Stoker's *Dracula* and Dennis Wheatley's Black Magic novels. At one stage he grew a toothbrush moustache and treated his fellows to a rousing impersonation of Hitler, many of whose speeches he knew in German by rote. He also developed a taste for Wagner, keeping the volume of the Broadmoor record-player as loud as possible.

Sedatives were meanwhile the only physical treatment he received. They changed his appearance noticeably, making him pale, fatter, more lethargic and occasionally slurring his speech. His family noticed this on one of their increasingly infrequent visits, and – apart from Fred – began to feel more pity than fear. Young told them he disliked the drugs, explaining their medical properties and effects. But his protests had been to no avail, and they were at times forcibly administered. Soon after this visit, Fred Young was asked to sign a form giving permission for Graham to undergo electro-convulsive therapy; he did so, but it seems unlikely that the treatment was ever administered. Broadmoor later refused to disclose the methods of treatment applied to Young, but evidence suggests they did not go beyond group therapy – which he shunned, finding the behaviour of other patients absurd – and special relationships with the two psychiatrists directly treating him.

These were the hospital superintendent, Dr Patrick McGrath, and a senior full-time psychiatrist,

Dr Edgar Udwin. Dr McGrath, as head of Broadmoor, was nominally responsible for every patient, but took a close personal interest in Young, especially during his early years in the hospital. Then he passed primary control to Udwin. Udwin was in his mid-fifties, Jewish, born in South Africa; he qualified at Witwatersrand University and joined the Broadmoor staff shortly before Young's arrival at the hospital. In his spare time, he ran a clinic for mentally handicapped children.

There is a long-standing rift at Broadmoor between the handful of senior staff psychiatrists and the nursing staff who supervise their patients from day to day. This is partly because the nurses are members of the Prison Officers Association. This has tended, they argue, to make some doctors undervalue their medical skills, identifying them more as the warders of conventional prisons than the qualified personnel they are. In turn, it makes some nurses feel that their written observations on patients, with whom they are in more regular contact, are not always consulted with the respect they merit. The files kept in the chief nurse's office, to which staff are obliged to add reports at regular intervals, occasionally contain judgements which are at odds with those of psychiatrists. For much of Graham Young's time in Broadmoor, his behaviour was too cooperative for doctors and nurses to have much to disagree about; at certain crucial stages, however, future action was the subject of bitter argument.

At the end of Young's first year in Broadmoor,

nurses were far from convinced that he was becoming a reformed, or even a mellowed, character. On the contrary, he remained either sullen or fractious. One nurse remembers: 'We had a lot of trouble with him in the beginning, and we had to put him on drugs to subdue him. That's not too unusual, as most patients suffer from depression when they first get here. But Young was different. He lived very much in a fantasy world at first, and we had a lot of trouble getting through to him. All he would talk about were his poisons. And this was the very subject we wanted to get him off, to channel his thoughts and energies into something else.'

But apart from the special observation maintained on so young a patient – one nurse has said he felt *in loco parentis* for the boy – Young was treated much the same as all other inmates during his years in the admission block. His movements outside the buildings were carefully restricted, and usually consisted of going down to the playing fields to watch a football or cricket match. He never himself joined in the game. This was not only because he was a far from natural sportsman; fellow inmates trying to befriend the boy were sometimes offended by his steadfast wish to be alone, his reluctance to join in any group activities despite the monotony of Broadmoor's daily routine. Handicrafts were really the only organized activity for newcomers, with breakfast, lunch and tea as the day's punctuation. Young spent the long hours expanding his collection of wooden and metal swastikas, wearing his favourite on a chain round his neck the while, occasionally kissing it with a wilful intent to outrage those around him.

Because of the publicity which had surrounded his arrival, and the way he quite simply – in one patient's words – 'put a lot of people's backs up', Young was the subject of spasmodic malicious rumours, all making play of his ability to extract poison from a stone. Several rather sick yarns found their way into the national papers, whose memories of the astonishing boy poisoner were still fresh. The *Daily Express* carried a light-hearted tale, which no-one at Broadmoor has ever denied: some of the patients were apparently getting drunk, though they of course had no access to alcohol; Young, it was explained, had been topping up cups of coffee with carbon monoxide from a gas-stove lighter.

Some patients lived in fear of the new recruit; others resented the star quality his youth and his notoriety won him. He was much more the centre of attention in Broadmoor than he had ever managed to be in Neasden. But the excitement of such a novelty patient soon wore off, and Young settled into the community quite amicably. In time, he made a few quite close friends; some former patients still, despite subsequent events, speak of him with a certain awe-struck admiration, if not altogether with warmth. The staff gradually felt reassured.

Nurses began to feel more confidence, and took their own private risk in his interests by appointing him to take charge of the kitchens in which their coffee and occasional meals were made. All went well until the not unexpected bitter-tasting, peculiarly dark cup of coffee was served. It turned out to contain Harpic. The nurses were sufficiently on their guard to avoid drinking any.

Despite being a passing object of his more unwelcome attentions, the nursing staff felt an unusual interest in Young, and tempered their anxiety with special efforts at friendship and understanding. There were periods when he was deliberately and ostentatiously treated as a popular character, to offset his unpopularity among the patients. Besides, in a light-hearted way (if with macabre overtones), Young was useful to the nurses. There were several occasions when they were able to avoid calling the physician on duty by consulting Young about the symptoms of some minor illness afflicting a patient. And he could be used as a handy threat; moments of mild rebellion could be quashed with a quiet: 'Unless you behave, I'll let Graham make your coffee in the morning.'

Young was all this time pursuing his familiar interests. Top of his reading list at this stage were *The Scourge of the Swastika*, Lord Russell's account of Nazi atrocities, and a study of Haigh, the acid bath murderer. But at the same time he was beginning to hatch plans for getting himself out of Broadmoor.

He made his first attempt at the end of his third year, 1965–6. Any patient in Broadmoor is entitled to apply for release to a review tribunal, which annually considers a number of applications, granting very few. Young filed his request, recognizing that the only other orthodox channels open to him – transfer to an ordinary mental hospital, or petitioning the Home Secretary to end his restriction order – looked less than promising. His father and Aunt Winifred were requested to attend the tribunal, all expenses paid, and remembered driving up from Sheerness through incongruously gay Ascot crowds. The board, five laymen and two psychiatrists, were left in no doubt of the family's wishes for Graham's future. Fred Young felt he should 'never be released again', adding that if he were he would not be given a home by any member of his family. Young's request for release was turned down.

His disappointment quickly deepened to resentment. A few months later, an alert patient noticed that one of the packets of sugar soap, used for cleaning the basins in the admission block wards, was missing from its place on a chest of drawers. The alarm was quickly raised, and the contents of the newly filled tea urn intercepted just at the start of the trolley's round. Analysis showed that the entire packet of sugar soap had been poured into the urn. Anyone drinking the tea would have had his stomach burnt out.

Young's poisoning campaigns outside Broadmoor were carefully planned. But the incidents inside the hospital[1] are more characteristic of the deranged poisoner so intent on his ends as to become stupidly

---

[1]Although Young's responsibility for these two attempts has never been brought to public proof, the confidential evidence of nursing staff and former patients is conclusive.

careless about means. The empty sugar soap packet was sitting on the lower tray of the tea trolley. The empty Harpic bottle was still standing on its shelf in the nurses' kitchen. The clumsiness of these Broadmoor attempts, granted that Young was hampered by a lack of his accustomed resources, make an intriguing counterpoint to his expertise outside. The last earned him a spell in the Broadmoor 'cooler' – the maximum security rooms of block six, where only the most violent patients are housed.

But the sugar soap incident was to be, as far as Broadmoor was concerned, Young's farewell to arms. He knew that good behaviour would above all be the key to an early release, and was careful not to blot his copybook again.

The self-restraint made him moodier than ever. 'If Graham didn't want to talk to you,' one nurse remembers, 'nothing would open him up. He'd tell you he wasn't prepared to talk, and then he'd just sit there, silently staring at you. No amount of questioning would draw him out. When you did get him talking, you had to be wary, as a lot of what he said would be lies.'

But he seemed prepared to be more forthcoming with his psychiatrists. Nurses recall that at first it had taken Dr Udwin a long time to get through to Young, but once the boy made his decision to co-operate, there seemed to be no problem. He began to make more friends, and took on responsibilities without abusing them. He even showed odd flashes of humour. As he buckled down more seriously to his studies, Udwin suggested he could still think in terms of a university place, offering Sussex as a tangible incentive. At the end of his fifth year in Broadmoor, Young was transferred to the less strict residential conditions of Block Two, and given increased freedoms within the hospital and its grounds. He was the model of good behaviour.

3

Entirely fit for discharge

Dear John,

I hope that you are keeping well. Just a few lines to let you know how I am getting on.

It is not too bad a place here. The food is pretty good, and there are things to occupy me some of the time. There is television to watch at night, and the wireless to listen to during the day. There is also billiards and snooker etc.

We can go down to the cricket field to watch the hospital playing an outside (or inside) team. I don't usually go down, though.

How are things with you? I get occasional reports about you from my 'spies' in Neasden. Dad saw you a couple of months ago with Richard, so he was telling me. You were in a place where I would very much like to have been.[1] Do you see anything of Jean nowadays? I have not heard from her for some time now . . .

My doctor here told me that I will not have to do fifteen years here. He has told me that if my progress continues I will be out in about six years.

[1] The local library.

This is still a long time but it is not half as long as fifteen years is it?

I have made some friends in here, but none as good as you were. We had our arguments and our setbacks, but we remained friends right up to the time that the trouble happened. I hope that we are still friends now.

Well, John, I will sign off now but I will write again soon.

I would be very pleased if you would reply to this letter as I would like to hear from you again . . .

All the best
your friend
Graham

Graham Young wrote that letter to his former friend Chris Williams (whom he knew by his second name, John) on 17 July 1963. He had been in Broadmoor just a year. And already, according to his evidence, Udwin was predicting a remarkably early release. Then came the fractious period, the various impulsive incidents, and the spell in the cooler – followed by Young's conscious decision to work for release. It took three long years of good behaviour to, in his own words, 'get things moving' at the Home Office.

They were difficult years for Young. He was perpetually taunted by jibes that he was becoming 'McGrath's blue-eyed boy'. Young ignored them, but they bore some truth. Udwin and McGrath consulted regularly about the boy who was fast becoming their star patient. Udwin's six-year prediction was over-ruled by the erratic behaviour of Young's early years in Broadmoor, but the two psychiatrists began after this spell of total co-operation seriously to re-consider the question of early release.

Although Mr Justice Melford Stevenson's order eight years before had specifically recommended a fifteen-year detainment, past experience had shown that recommendations from the superintendent and the responsible psychiatrist were sufficient to procure a release or transfer. Udwin and McGrath were especially aware at this stage that Young was approaching what some psychiatrists call the 'ten-year threshold'; after ten years in a hospital like Broadmoor, most patients are hopelessly insti-tutionalized, and beyond hope of ever recovering sufficiently from total care to be able to regain the independence necessary to survive outside. In the case of a patient still so young, humanitarian instincts prompted special attention to this problem.

The general air of optimism prompted Young to make a few preliminary postal sorties into the realms of future employment. Unknown to his psy-chiatrists, he applied for a job with the police forensic science laboratory, who despatched a prompt refusal. It is tempting to wonder if a more sympathetic reply might have changed the boy's future. But another curt rejection, this time to his request for details of the Pharmaceutical Society's training scheme and terms of membership, alienated him further. He slumped back into his old absorp-tions, and made another postal application – this time successfully. Young became a fully paid-up member of the Broadmoor branch of the National Front.

In June 1970 Udwin reported to the Home Office, as a preliminary step to recommending release on licence, that although Young had at first been slow to respond to treatment 'profound changes' had recently taken place. 'He is no longer obsessed with poisons, violence and mischief. And he is no longer a danger to others.'

Udwin told Young that his prospects looked good. He decided, meanwhile, to try out his new-found faith in the boy by allowing him a weekend visit to his family. Familiar with his father's steadfast resentment of Graham, Udwin suggested that he approach his sister Winifred, and ask if she'd be willing to have him for a few days. On 16 June, Graham wrote to her from Ward One, Kent House, Broadmoor, saying he had 'good news to import'. A conversation with 'the estimable Edgar' had revealed that things were moving at the Home Office, although no formal recommendation had yet gone in. They intended, however, to discharge him in the latter half of the year. 'The pot', Young told his sister, 'is now almost boiling. Just think, Win, another few months and your friendly neighbourhood Frankenstein will be at liberty once again.'

It was the first indication to any of the family that Young's release was even under consideration, let alone that it was imminent. A hurried consultation between Hemel Hempstead and Sheerness led to general dismay. But Winifred was determined to be forgiving; she agreed to give Graham his chance, and have him to stay.

She heard no more until October. Udwin had meanwhile again been in contact with the Home Office, and received a preliminary assurance that Young's case was under review. He approached Winifred with the news that he had been in touch with the Home Secretary, Reginald Maudling, about her brother, and that release might soon be possible. Would she, meanwhile, be prepared to have him for a week as a preliminary experiment?

Winifred's disconcerting conversation with her father had made her less sure. She asked for a personal interview with Udwin to allay any fears that Graham might not be completely cured. She now had, she pointed out, a baby to worry about. She and Dennis drove over to Broadmoor and saw the doctor personally. He gave her a full reassurance that there was no chance of Graham's reverting to his old habits. In mid-November she received a telegram from Udwin asking if a week's leave from 21 November would be convenient. On the appointed day, the Shannons again drove to Broadmoor, this time to give Graham his first taste of liberty for more than eight years.

The week was a great success. Winifred and Dennis, on Udwin's advice, had decided to trust Graham completely, rather than keeping eternal watch on him. He was given the free run of the house, including the kitchen, and seemed to respond gratefully. His familiar obsessions still dominated the conversation – at this stage he was studying the First World War – but there was scarcely a mention of poison. The only time it came up was in a candid few moments when the events of their childhood were quietly discussed. Graham professed great remorse, but was confident it would not happen again. Winifred in turn was convinced it had all been some mysterious kind of mental illness, now past. She was happy to see Graham get on so well with Dennis, and show such affection to their baby and their dog. A particular delight to all of them was Graham's discovery of the pub, an institution he was now fully appreciating for the first time in his life. To Dennis's surprise, Graham downed pint after pint with all the ease of an inveterate beer man.

Udwin was delighted by the favourable report he received from the Shannons on Graham's return a week later. The release date now seemed likely to be early in the New Year, and he suggested they might like to have Graham again for Christmas. They agreed.

Graham seemed even more normal at Christmas. Where on his previous visit he had been reserved, his conversation restricted, now he was full of gaiety and humour. Winifred thought he was becoming more accustomed to the kind of life eight years and more in Broadmoor had made him forget: a life, furthermore, he had known only as a child, never as the adult he seemed to have become. Graham again spent a lot of time with Dennis at the pub, cramming as much drinking as he could into the hours available. After a sequence of dismal

Decembers in Broadmoor, where Christmas is the worst of all times of year, he revelled in the celebration and present giving at Hemel Hempstead. He gave Dennis a book about Rommel, and presented a delighted Winifred with a lighter, a box of chocolates and a leather *Radio Times* cover. He even had a little present for their dog – a card, which he had inscribed:

To whom it may concern: This is to certify that Rupert Beagle has undergone psychoanalysis and, contrary to appearances, is not suffering from hydrophobia or any other canine psychosis.
Signed, Sigmund Freud

Young's taste of freedom made him exultant. He smoked incessantly now that cigarettes were available without restriction. He drank as heavily as time and money allowed. When he returned to Broadmoor, he was full of stories about Christmas in the normal world. He seethed with resentment at the years he had spent inside the hospital, and turned bitterly on all it stood for. Confident that he would soon be free, he was euphoric; obsessed by his wasted years, he was acidic. He lunged from one mood to the other like a manic depressive; and in one such moment, he told a nurse: 'When I get out, I'm going to kill one person for every year I've spent in this place.'

Udwin's recommendation for Young's release, backed by one from McGrath, sat in a file at the

Home Office's C3 division, responsible for Broadmoor admissions and discharges. Already in the C3 records was another file, detailing Young's early history and previous court appearance, and containing the reports made in 1962 by Doctors Fysh and Blair. The two files, like the two sets of reports, were never to meet.

Broadmoor's record at C3 was not flawless. Already in the files were the names of two of Udwin's patients who had been recommended for transfer, both of whom had subsequently returned to their violent ways – Billy Doyle and Marty Frape.

Martin Victor Frape was transferred from Broadmoor, where he had been sent for wounding, shopbreaking and sacrilege, to Parkhurst maximum security prison on the Isle of Wight. Udwin had advised that Frape, a twenty-eight-year-old psychopath with an emotional age of five, was more suited to serve his term in a conventional prison. But this was at a time in the mid-60s when Parkhurst was being overloaded with men of violent and unstable tendencies. Violence was a daily occurrence in the prison, which had no psychiatric facilities at all. On 24 October 1969 – three years to the day since the setting up of the Mountbatten inquiry, which had severely tightened up Parkhurst discipline – there occurred at the jail the worst riot in British prison history since the Dartmoor mutinies of the 1930s. Three of the riot's seven leaders were ex-Broadmoor patients. The one to receive the heaviest sentence in the ensuing trial – six years for holding a warder hostage at knife-point – was Marty Frape. 'I have a great deal of compassion towards you,' Mr Justice Bean told him. 'My tragedy and your tragedy is that I must protect society from the wildness of your ravings.'

William Thomas Doyle was sent to Broadmoor in April 1962, three months before Graham Young. He had been charged with grievous bodily harm, allegedly having struck a policeman on the head with a hammer, causing a wound that required eleven stitches. But the day before his trial, the Home Secretary, R. A. Butler, had ordered his detention at Broadmoor. In his first year at Broadmoor Doyle, then seventeen, was regarded as a very difficult case; he was said to have delusions, and to be under the impression that his food was being poisoned. In June 1963 he staged a thirty-one-hour rooftop siege, when he and another patient hurled slates at doctors and nurses pleading with them to come down; only the intervention of Doyle's mother persuaded him to call it off.

But in April 1966 Udwin recommended to Roy Jenkins, then Home Secretary, that Doyle be transferred to a conventional mental hospital; his behaviour had become 'amenable' and he was 'no longer a security hazard'. He was moved to Horton Hospital, Epsom. In his brief stay there, he proved too much for a conventional mental hospital to cope with; he became addicted to heroin through contact with other junkies in the hospital, he absconded frequently and perpetually caused trouble. Medical authorities at the hospital filed an official report that it was impossible to keep him there, and gave him an official discharge after one month.

In May 1967 Doyle was charged with, and admitted, murdering Antonio Cano Gonzales, a laundry worker at St Ebbas Hospital, Epsom. Doyle told police that he was in desperate need of heroin. He chased a friend with an iron bar in Paddington, took a taxi to Epsom and tried to attack the driver; then rang a bell at the nearest house and felled the householder when he came to the door. It was Gonzales, who died from sixteen blows to the head. Doyle stole a few pounds from the body and returned to Piccadilly to buy a few grains of heroin. He was later found suffering from an overdose in the public conveniences at Piccadilly underground station; from there he was taken to Charing Cross Hospital, where staff expressed surprise that he had survived. At a five-minute hearing at Lewes on 9 May 1967, Doyle was found unfit to plead to the charge of Gonzales' murder; he was returned to Broadmoor, where four months later he was found dead in a lavatory in the maximum security block. Another patient was subsequently convicted of his murder.

Udwin was praised in the press as 'Broadmoor's hero doctor' during Doyle's rooftop siege. He had tried to talk his patient down, and received a punch in the face for his trouble. But he had supervised many successful discharges from Broadmoor, whose recidivism rate is consistently low. His report on Young was sufficient to convince the Home Secretary's officers to disregard the 1962 warning that Young 'could repeat his cool, calm, calculating administration of these poisons at any time'.

There is no evidence that the 1962 file was even opened. Doctors Fysh and Blair were certainly never consulted. And it is known that the Home Office never saw the reports prepared regularly on Young, as on all patients, by the Broadmoor nursing staff. The nursing file on Young, which noted his vow to kill one person for each year he had spent in the hospital, never left the chief nurse's office. It remains confidential, but one of the nurses involved in compiling it has said:

'We were all against Graham's release. He made no secret of the fact that he intended to poison again. Indeed, he enjoyed boasting about his ambition to go down in history as the most famous poisoner since Crippen.'

Another nurse took a more sanguine view:

'There is an element of risk attached to the release of every patient. You can argue that there was no more of a risk with Graham as there is no known test you can give a poisoner to find out whether he will poison again. We knew there was a risk attached to Graham's release, but we'd never have let him out if we thought he'd repeat his actions, let alone if there was the remotest possibility of his poisoning again. I was convinced he would be all right.

'We were testing Graham for a full five years before he eventually got out. The nurses were making regular observation reports on him, and he was seeing his psychiatrist once a week. And then he was put through a whole battery of psychological tests.'

Broadmoor psychologists clearly have faith in their own testing system, although they have declined to specify what tests Young underwent. But a consultant psychiatrist comments: 'You can put a person through a whole range of psychological tests: test his intelligence, test his reactions, test practically anything. The only things these tests tell me is how the mind of the psychologist works.'

It is not unusual, or was not before Young's case, for the Home Secretary of the day to base a release decision purely on the recommendation of the psychiatrist in charge of the case. He does, however, have the option of asking any number of second opinions: notably that of the Mental Health Review Tribunal. This was not thought necessary in Young's case. Had he, however, been approached, this would have been the view of one member of the tribunal:

'You have two main factors: Young's views, and the boast he made. The fact that a person has anti-semitic views is obviously not in itself a reason for keeping him in a mental hospital. Yet what you have to consider here is that they are being expressed by a person with known aggressive tendencies. And there is another factor which rather complicates this issue: that Udwin himself is Jewish. I would imagine that being the sort of man he is he would have bent over backwards to be fair. But all the same this person is still extolling the virtues of exterminating Jews.

'Then there is the boast Young made. Let me put

Graham Young's favourite self-portrait, taken in a four-shot booth on Waterloo Station. Young himself sought its distribution to the press during his 1972 trial; the papers played it up as the portrait of a psychopathic killer. In fact the fearsome stare was captured by accident; Young was angry with the machine, which he thought had cheated him.

Graham Young in 1962, at the age of fourteen, when he was committed to Broadmoor for poisoning his father, his sister and a schoolfriend.

The terraced home at 768 North Circular Road, Cricklewood, London, where Young grew up, and in which he conducted his first poisoning campaign on humans – his family.

Graham Young's father, Fred, at the time of the 1962 trial, which sent his son to Broadmoor. Mr Young was still recovering from severe doses of antimony; he was never really able to forgive.

Young's Aunt Winnie, Winnie Jouvenat, who acted as his mother until his father remarried and always remained closer to him than anyone else in the family, and his sister, Winnie, named after her, who survived Young's poison attempts in 1962.

Tea lady Mrs May Bartlett with the trolley from which Young collected his workmates' individual cups; he dosed them with poison as he came back down the passage.

The photographic plant of John Hadland Ltd, at Bovingdon,
Hertfordshire, where Young poisoned four of his workmates,
two fatally.

Young's digs in Maynard Road, Hemel Hempstead, at the time
of his arrest.

Graham Young, the accused man, about to enter a police van.

On his way to court, Sir Arthur Irvine, QC for the defence.

Above. Bob Egle (left) and Fred Biggs, the two older men in the Hadland's storeroom who befriended Young, gave him cigarettes and lent him the bus fare home. He murdered them both.

Below. Jethro Batt (left) and David Tilson, two of Young's younger colleagues, who both lost all of their hair and were suicidal with pain after he poisoned them with thallium. He was convicted of attempting to murder them both.

Smoking, well-groomed and immaculately dressed, Young leaves Hemel Hempstead police station, handcuffed to an officer, to be remanded for the murder of Fred Biggs.

it this way: even if the remark was made as a joke, you still know that the thought was there in the first place. And it comes from a person, as I've said, with known aggressive tendencies. Quite clearly, he should never have been released.'

The tribunal member concedes, it should be added, that his views naturally benefit from hindsight. And it is unlikely that Young's vow ever reached the ears of any Home Office civil servant, or of the psychiatrists at Broadmoor.

It can never have got as far as the Home Secretary himself. It is indeed, on all the evidence, unlikely that Mr Maudling himself signed the release order. This was most probably done on his behalf by a junior minister. Maudling always refused to specify the extent of his involvement in the decision.

But the whole *raison d'etre* of a restriction order, always made by judges in respect of violent offenders, is to ensure that they are not released solely on the advice of their doctors. The Home Secretary's part in the process is therefore an indispensable one, and Maudling always accepted full responsibility for the decision to release Young.

The order was signed early in 1971, and a release date fixed for February. Three conditions were imposed: that Young reside at a fixed address, that he agree to undergo supervision by the probation service, and that he regularly attend a psychiatric out-patients clinic.

It is perhaps idle to speculate whether consultations with Dr Fysh and/or Dr Blair would have affected the decision. Their impressions of a

81

fourteen-year-old boy, for all the long-term conviction of their conclusions, may not have held true about Young during his teens and early twenties. But the fact is that the next poisoning charge he was to face dated from within a month of his release from Broadmoor; that his next sustained poisoning campaign constituted no more or less than a 'cool, calm, calculating administration of poison'; that for all the deliberateness of his vow, there is at best the eeriest of coincidences in the fact that after eight years in Broadmoor he was within the next twelve months to face eight charges of poisoning. When told, before the year was out, of the new set of charges against Young, Dr Fysh said: 'I am not surprised. I am no prophet, but I thought he would remain a permanent danger to the public for the remainder of his life.'

4

Catching up on lost time

On Thursday 4 February, Young stepped out of the
gates of Broadmoor. Free at last, he had four days
before starting at the Slough Training Centre, and
he decided to head for the familiar ground of
Winifred's home in Hemel Hempstead. No-one had
informed Fred Young down in Sheerness that his
son was being released; only Winifred had been
warned, and she herself was certain of nothing until
Graham turned up on her doorstep later that day.
She immediately wrote to tell her father of the news.
A month later a Broadmoor official knocked on Fred
Young's door and warned him that his son's release
was under discussion. Fred's answer was brief and
to the point; by then Graham had already been to
stay with him.

Young's behaviour during his weekend in Hemel
Hempstead was much as it had been at Christmas.
He left the house only to go to the pub with Dennis,
and again surprised his brother-in-law by the
amount of liquor he put back. At home he would
pace up and down lecturing the couple about the
First World War, about the sense behind Hitler's
ideas and about the British Government's feebleness

in dealing with the Ulster problem, then at one of its bloodiest stages. Young would, he told them, instigate immediate pogroms, sending the army in with every military device shown to science. Prime Minister Edward Heath should take a tip, he said, from the way Hitler sorted out Warsaw – erase the place systematically, block by block. That way many innocents would die, he granted that, but at least the IRA would be decimated. Winifred tried at first to disagree, but soon gave up. Graham was immune to argument.

That weekend he moved into the hostel in Bath Road, Cippenham, just six miles from the training centre. On Monday morning, 8 February, he punctually punched in clock-card number 497 at the Buckingham Avenue plant. Under the supervision of Mr W. E. James, Young began the routine and, to him, rather mindless course in store-keeping. As the weeks wore on, he proved himself a very willing and able trainee, more intelligent than the majority of those at the centre, particularly capable of working on his own or undertaking any special responsibilities offered to test him out.

Within days of arriving at the centre, Young struck up a friendship with another trainee, Trevor Sparkes, who had arrived a fortnight earlier and had a room near Young's in the hostel. The two would spend their evenings together at The Grapes in Slough, or drinking the wine which Young liberally dispensed after hours in his room at the hostel. Their conversations ranged from politics and history to music and, of course, medicine.

Thirty-four-year-old Sparkes, a keen amateur footballer, had suffered some sharp abdominal pains while on the pitch the week of Young's arrival. On 11 February, he took his troubles to a local GP, who could find nothing seriously wrong. But the pains continued, and on one afternoon when he had twice been sick, Sparkes asked Young what he – as a medical expert – thought the trouble might be. 'This might help,' said Young, offering him a glass of wine at the hostel that evening.

It didn't. Sparkes was violently sick during the night. He continued vomiting for four days, developed aches and pains in the groin, chronic diarrhoea and suffered what he called 'peculiar sensations' in the scrotum. Both sides of his face became swollen. He was taken to the training centre's sick bay, where he spent four days, and was prescribed milk of magnesia tablets. Sparkes re-started work when the worst of his pains eased and the vomiting stopped. But the abdominal trouble continued, and when next he played football he found himself losing control of his legs and thighs, until finally he had to leave the field. He has never played football since.

Six weeks later, after drinking more of Young's wine, the nausea and vomiting began again in earnest, and on 8 April Sparkes went back to the doctor, who diagnosed a urinary infection. Young continued the wine treatment, alternating it on occasions with water. Sparkes always found Young's attitude 'very sympathetic'. On 30 April, when both were about to leave the training centre,

Sparkes had butterflies in his stomach because of an interview that day with a prospective employer. He told Young, who gave him what he said was bromide to calm his nerves. He had bought it, he told Sparkes, especially for him from a chemist in Cippenham. Sparkes was violently sick.

The pains continued after he returned home to Welwyn Garden City. Sparkes continually felt tired and listless. His doctor was still baffled. After a further examination at Welwyn's Queen Elizabeth II Hospital on 11 June, the pain was diagnosed as probably due to a strain, and Sparkes was given a pain-killing injection. When the trouble continued, he was referred to a consulting physician, who diagnosed muscular trouble. On 6 December, eight months after Sparkes had left the training centre, samples of his blood and urine were taken as part of police investigations into Young. They revealed nothing abnormal.

At Young's trial the following July, Sparkes said he still suffered the same 'diabolical' pains. His football career had been ruined. It was the first time he had seen Young since both had left Slough; Sparkes looked at him more bitterly than did any other witness.

In the early April of 1971, Young began to make plans for his future. He immediately had an uncanny stroke of good luck: a vacancy for a storeman was being advertised by a small firm in the Hertfordshire village of Bovingdon, near his sister's home in Hemel Hempstead. The company was John Hadland Ltd, manufacturers of specialist high-speed optical and photographic instruments. Through the training centre's placing officer, Young applied. On the application form, under the section asking for 'any other relevant information', he wrote: 'I previously studied chemistry, organic and inorganic, pharmacology and toxicology over the last ten years, and I therefore have some knowledge of chemicals and their usage.'

On Saturday 17 April, the weekend after sending off his application, Young decided against spending the weekend with his sister in Hemel Hempstead or his father in Sheerness, as he had been in the habit of doing. Instead, he caught a train to London, and went straight to one of the capital's best-known chemists, John Bell and Croyden of Wigmore Street. He asked for a quantity of antimony potassium tartrate, but was refused it because he did not have the written authority necessary to purchase Schedule One poisons. Young tried to argue his case with an impressive run-down on the experiment he had in mind, as he had in his childhood, but the assistant was unimpressed. He left the store empty-handed.

The following Friday, 23 April, Young travelled to Bovingdon for his interview with the managing director of Hadland's, Mr Godfrey Foster. Mr Hadland himself, the company chairman, was then – as often – abroad on company business, and Mr Foster was seeing to the day-to-day running of the company. In front of him Mr Foster had two pieces of paper concerning his interviewee. (See page 89).

A glowing reference was signed by Young's supervisor, Mr James.

Mr Foster eyed the rather over-eager interviewee curiously. What had he done before going to the training centre? Young explained that he had had a nervous breakdown following the sudden death of his mother in a car accident, and had undergone mental treatment. But he was now quite recovered.

Young gushed about the usefulness of his scientific knowledge. Mr Foster was impressed, but unconvinced. He felt he should establish quite clearly that Young had recovered from his mental illness before firmly offering him the job. So he gave Young an encouraging word of farewell, and said he would let him know.

Young felt sure the job was in the bag. Next day, Saturday, he again caught the train to London and went to John Bell and Croyden. He asked, as he had seven days before, for twenty-five grams of antimony potassium tartrate. The assistant, Mrs Ruby Wooding, called over the senior dispenser, Mr Albert Kearne, who always dealt with requests for Schedule One poisons. Mr Kearne asked the customer for his authorization, which he produced. It was a sheet of printed notepaper, headed Bedford College, London, giving handwritten authority for M. E. Evans to purchase the antimony he required. Mr Kearne formed the impression that this slim young man 'of scholarly appearance' was probably a medical student engaged on research. Young confirmed that he needed the poison for scientific experiment and signed the poison register:

TRAINEE'S PLACING REPORT

SLOUGH

GTC or training establishment :

Name .... YOUNG, G. F. .... Clock no. 497 Age 23 Month/Single

Training trade .... Ind. Storekeeping .... Date of entry 8.2.71

Details of training are shown overleaf. Observations to assist in placing (particular ability, special qualifications, etc.) are as follows:

This man has an above average intelligence. He is very conscientious in his work, able to work to instructions given to him as well as on his own initiative. The ability to use shown in understanding the various aspects of storekeeping will prove him an asset to any future employer. His timekeeping and general behaviour have been excellent.

TFM 191   V B JONES

Staff ....

T45

Department of Employment and Productivity
Government Training Centre
119-122 Buckingham Avenue Slough Bucks

Telephone 23326

Your reference

Mr Foster   Our reference
John Hadiaru (Photographic
           Instrumentation) Ltd   Date 20 April 1971
Newhouse Laboratories
Newhouse Road
BOVINGDON, Herts.

Dear Sir

Further to our conversation of 20 April 1971, I am
forwarding herewith the placing report concerning
Mr Young, who will be coming to see you on Friday next
at 2.30 p.m.

I am also enclosing some literature which will explain
more fully the functions of the Government Training Centre
and their services to industry.

Thanking you for your kind consideration.

            I am
            Yours faithfully

                J R Ayles

                J H AYLES

JHA/EH

89

![Department emblem] **Department of Employment and Productivity**
Government Training Centre
119-122 Buckingham Avenue Slough Bucks

Telephone 23326

Mr Foster
Messrs John Hadland (Photo
Instrumentation) Ltd
New House Laboratories
New House Road
BOVINGTON, Herts.

Your reference

Our reference

Date 26 April 1971

Dear Sir

In response to your request I am forwarding a copy of Dr Unwin's report on Mr Young. I am sure you will find this satisfactory.

Yours faithfully

J R AYLES

JRA/BJ

---

15 January 1971

Medical Certificate
Graham Frederick YOUNG

This man has suffered a deep going personality disorder which necessitated his hospitalisation throughout the whole of his adolescence. He has, however, made an extremely full recovery and is now entirely fit for discharge, his sole disability now being the need to catch up on his lost time.

He is capable of undertaking any sort of work without any restrictions as to residence, travel or environment. His natural bent is towards the non-manual and clerical and in the first instance he would do extremely well training as a store keeper. He is of above average intelligence and capable of sustained effort. He would fit in well and not draw any attention to himself in any community.

(E L Unwin)
Consultant Psychiatrist

90

Slough. G.I.E.
Bath Road,
Slough.
April 28th 1971.

Mr. Forster,
Newhouse Laboratories, Ltd.,
Bovingdon.
Dear Mr. Forster,

Thank you for your letter of the 26th inst., in which you offer me the post of asst. Storekeeper.

I am pleased to accept your offer, and the conditions attached thereto, and shall, therefore, report for work on Monday, May 10th, at 8.30 a.m

May I take this opportunity to express my gratitude to you for offering me this position, notwithstanding my previous infirmity as communicated to you by the Placing Officer. I shall endeavour to justify your faith in me by performing my duties in an efficient and competent manner.

Until Monday week, I am,
Yours faithfully,
Graham Young.

91

M. E. Evans, 23 Denzil Road, Willesden, and slipped the authorization back in his pocket. Chemists are required by law to attach the written authority to the relevant entry in the poison register. Seven months later, the police were to ask John Bell and Croyden to produce this authority, and Mr Kearne was to have to admit in court that extensive searches had failed to reveal it.

Back in Slough, Young started his penultimate week at the training centre. Mr Foster of Hadland's, meanwhile, had recontacted Mr Ayles and asked for further reassurance about Young from the psychiatrist who had treated him during his mental illness. The Slough authorities were keen that Young, one of their star products, should get this job, and responded quickly. By Monday morning, Mr Ayles had forwarded to Foster a copy of a report sent by Dr Udwin (misspelt as Unwin in the report), adding that he was sure he would find it satisfactory. (See page 90.)

Foster was entirely satisfied. He wrote at once to Young offering him the job. Two days later, on 28 April, Young replied from the Bath Road hostel. (See page 91.)

Young left Slough on Friday, 8 May. The training centre's general manager, forty-four-year-old Mr Ernest Nicholls, gave him another glowing reference: 'A very good trainee, very keen and industrious, he has made satisfactory progress and successfully completed his course. I have no complaints at all about his behaviour.' With it went a certificate to the effect that Young had passed a Government training course in storekeeping.

Slightly less glowing was the account of Young's behaviour at the training centre from a fellow trainee, Henry Tennant, of Littlemore, Oxfordshire, who was training as a motor mechanic while Young was in Slough. 'Young kept to himself and rarely spoke. A bit moody, we thought. If I'd known about Broadmoor, it might have explained all the tummy upsets I suffered at Slough. Quite a few of us went down with a mystery bug. Knowing what we all know now, it makes you wonder.' There is no evidence to suggest that Young was responsible for any illnesses suffered by Slough trainees or management while he was there. He was even acquitted of poisoning Sparkes at his trial the following year; subsequent events were to take the emphasis off Sparkes's complaints. Police found sufficient evidence to support charges but not to win a conviction.

Young's sister Winifred had agreed to put her brother up for as long as he needed while he settled down to his new life in Hemel Hempstead. But he spent this weekend, the last before starting his new job, down in Sheerness with his father and his Aunt Winnie. Despite several weekend visits from Slough, Fred Young was still not entirely accustomed to the fact of his son's freedom, nor prepared to forgive and forget quite so readily as the rest of the family. The permanent damage suffered by his liver and other internal organs in 1962 left him with a considerable grudge, but he could never dismiss the bitterness he felt about the loss of his second wife.

Aunt Winnie insisted that Graham be given a chance to prove himself, which meant allowing him to have free run of the house – including the kitchen – without undue anxiety or interference. Fred was unsure, but agreed for the boy's sake. He rarely spoke to Graham nor Graham to him. 'They were more like total strangers than father and son,' recalled Aunt Winnie. Yet not once during those visits, nor those that followed in the coming months, was there any suggestion that Young tampered with food or drink in any way. There was no illness at the Sheerness home. Graham was very talkative and lively. Winnie sensed that Fred Young was still nervous of his son, if not positively afraid of him; but she was equally confident that Graham's behaviour proved what the doctors had told her: he was completely recovered.

Young started work at Hadland's at eight thirty a.m. on Monday 10 May. He continued to live with Winifred and Dennis for the first few weeks, but was encouraged by his probation officer to find a place of his own. The probation service's policy for those on parole is to promote complete independence of family or other ties so far as day-to-day self-sufficiency is concerned. It was important that Young be near some members of his family, but equally important that he relearn how to live his own life. So Young looked around for a place of his own in Hemel Hempstead, and finally saw an advert in the window of a newsagent in The Marlowes, Hemel Hempstead's main shopping street.

It directed him to 29 Maynards Road, a semi-detached house in a quiet residential street parallel to The Marlowes, close both to the town centre and to his sister's home in the more select suburb of Leverstock Green. A small bedsitter was on offer at four pounds a week. Young knocked on the bright mauve front door, and was shown upstairs by the houseowner, Mr Mohammed Saddiq, a West Pakistani. He took the room at once.

Although Mr Saddiq and his family spoke little English, over the following weeks they enjoyed a friendly relationship with their tenant, who never caused any trouble. It was one of the rules of the house that tenants were not allowed to do their own cooking, nor use the Saddiq family kitchen, so Young was free of temptation. He ate all his meals out, mostly at a nearby Wimpy bar, and twice a week – usually on Thursdays and Saturdays – at Winifred's.

He contented himself, meanwhile, with amassing his own infernal kitchen in the tiny room at the top of the stairs. He lined the cupboards and window-sills with his steadily increasing collection of drugs and poisons, and he decorated the walls with pictures of Nazi leaders. By the bed he kept a collection of books on poisons and forensic medicine, borrowed from the public library across the main road.

It was during these first few weeks of his new life that Young paid a sentimental visit to Neasden, revisiting all his old haunts. He tried to see his former headmaster at John Kelly School, but found that he had retired. He went instead round the corner from the old family home to visit his Uncle Frank. Then he took a long look at the small terraced house in the North Circular Road which was the scene of his earlier crimes, and boldly knocked on the door of a neighbour. He had to explain who he was, and then spent some time convincing his parents' old friends that he was not on the run from Broadmoor. 'Here, have you got over the wall?' they asked. 'No,' he kept telling them, 'they've let me out, they've let me out.' He rounded off his afternoon with a visit to the chemist's shop where he had bought poisons as a teenager by the name of M. E. Evans. This time he bought a tube of toothpaste.

There had been two conditions to Young's parole from Broadmoor: that he visited Dr Udwin's clinic in Reading regularly, and that he agreed to undergo supervision by the probation service in whatever area he moved to. In the event of his moving an inconvenient distance from Reading, the first condition was to be met by regular contact with Udwin, and attendance at the out-patients unit of a local psychiatric clinic, or the psychiatric wing of a local hospital.

During his thirteen weeks in Slough, Young paid three routine visits to a local psychiatric consultant, who reported back to Udwin. Before leaving the training centre, he had two telephone conversations with Udwin, who was very pleased with his progress. Once Young moved to Hemel Hempstead, they had no further contact.

When Young moved from Broadmoor to Slough, the Thames Valley police were informed about the poisoner on their patch. When Young moved from Slough to Hemel Hempstead, Hertfordshire police received no notification.

Young was conscientious about his weekly visits to Hemel Hempstead's probation office. In accordance with probation service policy, which insists on discretion about past convictions, his supervisor never visited either Young's place of work or his digs. Young's bedsitter laboratory in Maynards Road was also his place of sanctuary.

In the days before the arrival and rapid expansion of Hemel Hempstead new town, Newhouse Farm looked out from the edge of Bovingdon village across a rolling expanse of meadowland. Still a picturesque rural village, Bovingdon naturally took in evacuee children from London during the Second World War; but its rural calm was rudely shattered one night when a stray German bomber dropped its load on the fields of Hertfordshire, twenty-five miles north of the capital. Newhouse Farm suffered a direct hit. Miraculously, the farmer and his sixteen evacuees were unhurt, while the farm buildings were extensively damaged. The War Damage Commission rebuilt the farm after the war, but on the day of completion in 1948 an old man living in the village hanged himself from an apple tree in the grounds. The effect on the village was so powerful that no-one went near the place for seventeen years.

Then in 1965 John Hadland, who with his wife Daphne had been running a growing photographic equipment business from their nearby home, bought the farm and adapted it for use as a laboratory. They added prefabricated buildings for storage and production units. Undeterred by the local curse on the farm, the company thrived and in 1966 knew its finest hour with the marketing of the Imacon camera, the world's fastest, capable of taking sixty million pictures a second. It earned them a place in the Guinness Book of Records.

The staff of Hadland's and the villagers of Bovingdon were to be given good reason to remember that curse by the smart young man who caught the bus from his Hemel Hempstead digs to the Newhouse Laboratory on the morning of 10 May 1971. Graham Young, newly appointed £24-a-week assistant storeman, was given a warm welcome.

Young's workmates in the storeroom at Hadland's were a cheery group who quickly befriended the new recruit despite his eccentric and sometimes rather curt behaviour. They found him very quiet, somewhat absent-minded, often very distant and above all quite unpredictable – one day he would brightly join in the regular office banter, the next he would scarcely speak to anyone. He would often spend the morning and afternoon breaks sitting alone, reading rather impressive books about medicine, about war, about famous murderers. The only time he really came to life was when he could buttonhole someone and start a heated conversation about chemistry or politics – his favourite topic being Adolf Hitler.

One man his own age with whom he had many long conversations was Martin Hancock, who worked as a technical assistant at Hadland's for twelve months before leaving in September 1971 to go to college. 'I had many long conversations with Young, mostly about pharmacy and chemistry,' Hancock recalled. 'I remember we had both read Shirer's book about the Third Reich, which we discussed at great length.' Hancock was 'greatly surprised' at the amount Young knew about chemicals, and the fluency with which he could reel off names and properties. He found Young 'completely emotionless, except for his rather dry sense of humour'. Young told him he did not enjoy his work in the storeroom, and that he often felt the people there were getting on top of him.

Young's closest colleague at first was forty-one-year-old Ron Hewitt, a storeman-cum-driver who was shortly to leave, and whose storeroom duties Young had been hired to take over. Hewitt took pains to show Young the ropes and found him 'perfectly pleasant, if a bit baffling'. Their boss in the storeroom was fifty-nine-year-old Bob Egle, a benevolent family man looking forward to his approaching retirement. He and his wife Dorothy had been married thirty-eight years, and were planning to move when he retired from their home in Chesham to live near their married daughter in Gillingham, Norfolk. Egle was a Dunkirk veteran, and found that Young could never hear enough about his wartime experiences. The other senior

member of the staff was sixty-year-old Frederick
Biggs, boss of the Work In Progress department,
which stocked and issued parts for distribution to
the assembly section. Biggs worked part-time at
Hadland's, being already semi-retired after years
running the village stores in the nearby village of
Chipperfield, where he and his wife still lived. He
and his wife Annie had once been ballroom dancing
champions, and were still keen enthusiasts. For five
years Fred Biggs had represented Chipperfield on
Hemel Hempstead rural council.

The two elderly men felt almost parental responsibility for Young, so incapable did he seem of
keeping his life in order. They would often lend him
cigarettes, or money for his bus fare home. Young
always repaid his debts, and occasionally would
reward some act of generosity with one of his own
scraggy roll-up cigarettes, which they noticed he
held between his thumb and index finger, so that
his thumb was heavily stained with nicotine. After
a while Jethro Batt, thirty-nine-years-old and
another assistant storeman, took to giving Young a
lift back into Hemel Hempstead after work each
night. Young responded to their kindness by
volunteering to fetch everyone's tea from the trolley
brought round each day by Mrs May Bartlett. Mrs
Bartlett stopped her trolley at the end of the passage
outside, so fetching the tea was a chore they were
happy to leave to him.

Apart from a few twists and turns, a long corridor
runs straight down the length of the Newhouse
Laboratories, both old and new buildings. At its far

end is a half-door connecting Fred Biggs's Work In Progress section with the storeroom, beyond which is the packing department where Graham Young did most of his work checking in raw materials and packing finished work for despatch. It was along this corridor that Mrs Bartlett wheeled her trolley, stopping at the door of each department for employees to fetch their tea. When she came to the storeroom she would call out, and the volunteer took a tray to fetch the tea. Everyone had their own individual mug, clearly marked. Between the tea trolley and the storeroom, whoever was fetching the tea was out of sight of his workmates for several moments.

On Thursday 3 June, less than a month after Young had joined Hadland's, the store-room boss, Bob Egle, was taken ill. He went back to his home in Whelpley Hill, just outside Chesham, with very bad diarrhoea. It continued all through the next day, and he was laid up in bed over the weekend. On Monday 7 June he was well enough to return to work.

But next day it was Ron Hewitt's turn to feel ill. Soon after drinking a cup of tea fetched by Young, he too developed diarrhoea, accompanied by sharp stomach pains. The pains soon became worse, and Hewitt began to vomit. There was a fierce burning sensation at the back of his throat. He went straight home to Tedder Road, Hemel Hempstead. Next day, when all the symptoms persisted, he went to his GP, who diagnosed a severe chill or some kind of food poisoning. On the two following days, Thursday and

101

Friday, the vomiting, stomach pains and diarrhoea all persisted, and the burning in his throat became worse. On both days he visited his doctor, but nothing he was given eased the trouble. After a week he went back to work. The worst of the symptoms had let up, but he was still very fragile. During the next three weeks he suffered twelve more bouts of severe sickness and diarrhoea, often after drinking tea. He was on and off work 'like a yo-yo'.

Bob Egle, meanwhile, still didn't feel quite himself. On Friday 18 June he and his wife decided to take a week by the sea at Great Yarmouth. The Biggses were at the time on a fortnight's holiday in Tossa de Mar, so the storeroom was rather short-staffed. The others noticed how Young tended to try and take charge of things.

On Friday 25 June, two days before Bob Egle was due back from holiday, Young went again to John Bell and Croyden, and returned to his bedsitter for the weekend with twenty-five grams of thallium in his pocket. Thallium is a tasteless, odourless, colourless, soft metallic element, never before used in Britain as a means of murder. Its best known use was as a rat poison, but availability was strictly controlled in this country after it was found that the poison could be ingested through the pores of the skin, and that simply touching it could be fatal. It has occasionally been used as a depilatory agent on children, but the dangers involved made doctors use it only in extreme circumstances. In other countries, especially Australia and the Low Countries, the lack of legal control has led to a number of thallium murders. It was used in Holland during the last war as a means of disposing of occupying Nazis, the best known example being the murder of all the controllers of an arms factory when the work force put thallium into the water supply.

Its main industrial use is in the manufacture of optical lenses of a high refractive index – exactly the work carried on at Hadland's. There is some irony in the fact that the Slough placement officer was content for Young, a convicted poisoner who had used thallium, to obtain a job in a photographic laboratory; much more ironic, however, is the fact that no thallium at all was stocked at Hadland's while Young was working there. He had to buy it all from a chemist twenty-five miles away in central London, as he did that Friday evening in June 1971.

The following Monday Bob Egle was back at work in good spirits, feeling much better for his week by the sea. 'Back in top shape,' he told his colleagues. 'Nothing like a bit of sea air.'

Next day he took a dramatic turn for the worse. He felt so ill he couldn't work, and went straight home. He told his wife that his fingers had all gone numb at the ends. She gave him a cup of tea, and he lay down on the sofa. He could eat no dinner. That evening his wife suggested some fresh air, so they decided to take a walk down the road to look at their daughter's horse. But Egle didn't get very far. He started staggering like a drunk. His wife helped him back home and took him upstairs to bed.

Egle couldn't feel his tie or the buttons on his shirt, so she helped him undress. He got into bed at nine

103

p.m., but didn't sleep at all. Throughout the night he kept groaning because of a violent backache. The weight of the sheets caused him intolerable pain. At six a.m. he told his wife he could not feel his feet, so she called the doctor, who gave her two white tablets for her husband. Egle couldn't keep them down. His wife called the doctor again. He decided that Bob Egle had peripheral neuritis, and must be immediately admitted to hospital.

Mrs Egle travelled with her husband in the ambulance to the West Herts Hospital, Hemel Hempstead. By the time they arrived the pain in his back was so intense he was reeling from side to side. Next day he was transferred to the intensive care unit at St Albans City Hospital, twelve miles away. His condition grew steadily worse each day, as the paralysis which had started at his fingertips gradually spread through his entire body. A sign over his bed told visitors that he could hear what they said to him but could not reply. His wife spent all her time at his bedside. Twice his heart stopped beating, but both times the intensive care unit team – led by Dr Roger Gulin, medical registrar – managed to revive him. Then on Wednesday 7 July, after eight days of increasingly intense pain, Bob Egle died.

Graham Young had been very concerned about Egle's illness. Every day his boss was in hospital, Young would go upstairs at Hadland's to see the managing director's secretary, Mrs Mary Berrow, and ask how Egle was getting on. On one occasion, apparently trying to help, he showed her a highly technical article in *The Lancet* on the subject of polyneuritis. He pointed out to Mrs Berrow that the symptoms described in the article were very like those of the two men who had been taken ill at Hadland's. But Mrs Berrow couldn't understand a word.

The seventy-five members of the Hadland's staff were shaken by Egle's death. On Friday 9 July, two days after the storeroom boss had finally died, Ron Hewitt left – not without a feeling of relief. He still felt 'a bit shaky', but the attacks had eased of late. Five months later, when Hewitt learnt the true reason for Egle's death, he spent a few weeks feeling uneasy, for he remembered that he had often found the tea brought him by Young rather bitter, and had left it after one or two sips; Egle, always a man with something of a thirst, often used to finish it off for him.

On the same day that Hewitt left Hadland's, a post-mortem was performed on Egle, but no satisfactory explanation for such extensive paralysis could be found. Death was certified as being due to broncho-pneumonia, in conjunction with a little-known syndrome, Guillain-Barré polyneuritis. These facts were entered on Egle's death certificate and permission was given to go ahead with the burial. An inquest was not thought necessary.

The funeral service and cremation were arranged for the following Monday. Several members of the Hadland's staff asked Mr Foster, the managing director, if they might attend. Foster decided that 'the most satisfactory arrangement' would be for himself to represent the company, and to take along a member of the storeroom staff who had worked under Egle. He chose the man who seemed to have been closest to Egle, and whom he intended to succeed him as head of the storeroom – Graham Young.

Young sat next to Foster during the funeral service at Whelpley Hill's tiny parish church. The two then drove in Foster's car to the cremation ceremony at Amersham. On the way, Young seemed eager to talk about Egle's death. He asked Foster if he knew yet what had been the cause. Foster told Young he had that morning received a copy of the death certificate, which had named polyneuritis.

'But polyneuritis is only a general term, meaning that whatever it was affected the entire nervous system,' said Young. 'Surely there must have been some more detail on the death certificate?'

Foster said he thought it was a French-sounding name. 'It sounds to me like the Guillain-Barré syndrome,' said Young. Foster remembered the name when he heard it, and told Young he was quite right.

Young grew enthusiastic. 'It's a relatively new discovery,' he told Foster. 'The complaint has only recently been isolated. A number of treatments are being tried.'

He went on to describe in detail the nature of the syndrome and the remedies currently under investigation. Every word went well over Foster's head. He was 'deeply impressed by the extent of the young man's knowledge', but he was unable to remember a word later in the year. He could not forget, however, what Young said as they drove up to the crematorium: 'It's very sad that Bob should have come through the terrors of Dunkirk, only to fall victim to some strange virus.'

After the cremation, where they both paid their respects to Egle's widow, Foster drove Young back to Bovingdon. All the way, Young talked about the causes of Egle's death and the nature of his illness. He explained that polyneuritis must have been the first thing to strike Egle, that this would gradually have caused broncho-pneumonia, and that broncho-pneumonia would have been the actual cause of death. Foster was again reminded of what he had read on the death certificate, and confirmed every word. He remembers feeling 'very, very surprised' by the depth of Young's medical knowledge.

No-one at Hadland's saw any reason, amid all the speculation and gossip, to link Bob Egle's sudden and mysterious death with the illness of Ron Hewitt. Now that he too was gone, there seemed to be no further illness at the plant. For the next two months, life at Hadland's was uneventful; the place seemed to have got back to normal. One reason may be that it was during these two months that Graham Young took his summer holiday, during which he visited his father and aunt in Sheerness, and his cousin Sandra in St Albans.

When he returned to the storeroom, Young was put in charge for a probationary period. He tended to boast about the responsibility rather than exercise it. He seemed livelier, more excitable than when he had first joined, and everyone noticed how much more outgoing he had become in recent weeks. More than anyone he would talk regretfully of Bob Egle's death; he seemed to keep raising the subject even when it was clear that no-one else much wanted to talk about it. But for all that he was growing generally more popular, some still regarded him with a degree of caution; he had strange habits, such as a delight in killing insects with fly spray and a *penchant* for working without the lights on after dark. His conversational obsessions remained much the same.

But the more open-minded staff members were also struck by an unprecedented interest in others, and a new generosity. When Fred Biggs, a keen gardener, kept complaining about the insects that were ruining his flowers and shrubs, Young offered to help. They had already put their heads together to cope with a plague of wasps in the storeroom, and had adopted Young's suggestion of attracting them away by placing bowls of sugared water at strategic positions outside. Young used to enjoy watching them drown. Now he asked Biggs whether he had ever tried nicotine as an anti-insect measure. Biggs said he hadn't, so that week Young bought some nicotine in Hemel Hempstead and took it to work for Biggs. He was a bit annoyed to find that Biggs was unimpressed by the idea; he turned down the nicotine, and Young had to take it back home with him. He was meanwhile proving a none too efficient storeroom boss; he could scarcely keep his own work in order. Fred Biggs was ready with suggestions about improving the system; Young accepted them with bad grace.

But he still insisted on solving Fred Biggs's gardening problem. Young knew nothing about gardening, he told Biggs, but he felt certain his knowledge of chemicals could help. He suggested that a solution of thallium – some ten grams to a gallon of water – might prove an effective insecticide. Biggs didn't argue. Young gave him fifteen grams of thallium, warning him that it should never be handled without gloves on. Biggs took the thallium home, but never told Young if it proved successful – or indeed if he ever used it. The subject was never again mentioned.[1]

The summer weeks passed placidly enough. Young still visited his sister and brother-in-law in Leverstock Green, usually on Thursday evenings for a drinking session, and on Saturdays for the 'decent meal' his sister felt she should give him. His friendship with his cousin in St Albans, Sandra Lynn, became closer; he had never really had a chance to know her before, and he took to visiting her most weekends. He also went down to Sheerness regularly, and his father and aunt were delighted by the success at work of which he told them. He also told all his family about Egle's death, and about the other illnesses at the plant, but it never occurred to any of them to think twice about such things. All were appropriately remorseful when the truth was eventually revealed.

---

[1]Medical evidence at Young's trial ruled out the possibility of Biggs's having used this thallium, or even having opened the packet.

The calm at Hadland's was rudely shattered early in September, when Fred Biggs suddenly began to experience violent stabbing pains in his stomach, and to vomit copiously. He and his wife were due to go on a touring holiday round Britain that weekend – and when Sunday came he did in fact feel well enough to go. On Monday 20 September he was back at work, feeling fine. But that very day, the firm's import-export manager, Peter Buck, developed exactly the same symptoms fifteen minutes after having a cup of tea with Young and David Tilson, an import-export clerk. First came the headache, then the feelings of nausea. He sat down for a moment, then rushed off to be violently sick. Tilson took him home.

The next day Buck was back at work. He noticed Young reading a book and asked him what it was. 'It's about man's preoccupation with death,' Young told him. Buck told Young, perhaps with unconscious logic, that it was the tea which had made him so ill the day before; he knew that because he had had no breakfast, and the vomit had consisted of tea only. But Buck felt quite better, and was never ill in that way again. Less than three weeks later, however, it was Tilson's turn. On Friday 8 October, he felt a bit queasy after his morning tea break, but well enough to continue work. Next day, Saturday, he felt pins and needles in his feet. They would not go away.

When they continued through the night into Sunday, Tilson began to get worried. His legs were slowly going completely numb. On Monday morning he was no better, and went with difficulty to see his doctor. He was told to rest; and as the day progressed the numbness ebbed, causing the pain to return. On the Tuesday he was back at work, feeling physically better but generally apprehensive. His legs were still rather stiff.

Three days later, on Friday evening, Jethro Batt and Young were alone together in the stores, working later than the others. This was quite normal: Batt liked to work late to let the rush hour subside before driving home to Harrow. Young would work on as well so that Batt could drop him off at home on his way through Hemel Hempstead.

Young's conversation that evening was almost entirely morbid, but that was nothing new. 'Do you know, Jeth,' he said, 'it is quite easy to poison someone and make it look like natural causes.' He proceeded to give Batt what he called his 'recipe for death' and to suggest ways in which it could be administered. What followed would suggest that Batt was extremely simple-minded not to realize Young's guilt; he admitted as much privately some months later, saying he had always thought Young 'a bit rum', but had 'just failed to put two and two together'.

Batt left his bench for a moment to go to the lavatory. When he returned Young was waiting for him with a cup of coffee. It looked rather dark. Batt tasted it and found it bitter. Being particular about his coffee, he drank only the one mouthful and then poured it away, telling Young he didn't think much of it.

'What's the matter?' Young asked. 'Do you think I'm trying to poison you?' Both men laughed. It was a natural joke after Young's 'recipe for death'.

Twenty minutes later Batt was back in the lavatory, being violently sick. He decided to call it a day, and gave Young a lift home.

Over the weekend Batt felt 'dodgy'. He noticed an increasingly severe pain in both legs. Meanwhile, David Tilson woke up on Saturday morning feeling 'not completely all right'. By Sunday his pins and needles had returned, while Batt's legs had gone numb and the pains had moved to his stomach.

On Monday morning, 18 October, both men went to their doctors. Tilson had pains in his chest and stomach, and could not breathe properly. A deep breath was extremely painful. His legs, knees and ankle joints were stiff; he still had pins and needles in his feet. His doctor gave him some more pills. Batt had agonizing leg pains.

The next day Tilson felt much worse, after a sleepless night. His bedclothes had caused him great pain. He went again to his doctor, who arranged for him to be admitted to St Albans City Hospital for observation. He continued to vomit, but began to feel a little better. Then his hair started to fall out.

That day, Tuesday, Batt's pains moved up from his legs to his chest and stomach. He stayed at home in bed. At Hadland's, meanwhile, Mrs Diana Smart – a wire-woman who occasionally helped out in the storeroom – had a cup of coffee with Young, with whom she had been spending quite a lot of time. He had brought it to her desk, saying: 'This is your coffee, Di. Drink it up.' She began to be sick, developed stomach and leg pains, pins and needles in her hands, then cramp. She went straight home.

Next day, Jethro Batt told his wife he wanted to kill himself. The pain was fearful. His hair had begun to fall out. He was having terrifying hallucinations. His wife thought she had 'lost him to some kind of mysterious madness'. Tilson was still in hospital, feeling much worse. Diana Smart was at home in bed.

On Thursday morning Batt woke up to find himself unable to move. He shifted slowly, painfully, but could not get out of bed. His toes were painful and completely rigid. He was to stay in bed at home until 5 November, when he was finally admitted to the West Herts hospital in Hemel Hempstead. His head was completely bald, and he was dangerously suicidal. Since the pains had begun on 15 October, he had been impotent.

Tilson, meanwhile, remained in St Albans City Hospital until 28 October. He was not by then recovered, but his condition had stopped deteriorating sufficiently for him to go home. Besides, doctors were suspicious that he was a malingerer, and that his unusual symptoms – which could be accounted for individually, but not in conjunction – were to some degree psychosomatic. At home, his hair began to fall out in chunks. When he climbed the stairs or even walked down the hall, he noticed his pulse and heart rate increase considerably. He called his doctor and went straight back to bed.

By the end of the weekend he was feeling worse

than ever. On Monday morning, 1 November – just four days after his discharge – he was readmitted to St Albans City Hospital. He had left with shoulder-length hair and a heavy beard; when he returned, doctors described him as looking like 'a three-quarter plucked chicken'. Most of his head, face and body hair was completely gone; only odd tufts remained. He took to wearing a wig. Something of a ladies' man, he too had found himself totally impotent for almost a month.

That weekend had been an eventful one at Hadland's. It was annual stocktaking time, and with Tilson and Batt off sick, and Egle still unreplaced, staff were putting in a lot of overtime. In charge of the storeroom was the only full-time member still on his feet, Graham Young. He went in on the Saturday, and both Fred Biggs and his wife came in to help, despite the fact that Fred had been off work several days that week with further bouts of sudden, violent sickness.

Young had made special arrangements to have Mrs Bartlett's key to the tea cupboard over the weekend so that he could keep his helpers well supplied. The cupboard was normally kept locked, and keys restricted with almost uncanny caution; but extra weekend working was reason enough to relax the rules. Both morning and afternoon on the Saturday Young made tea for the Biggses, which they drank with him. Mr Foster came in during the afternoon to see how things were going. Young offered to make him a cup of tea, and he accepted gratefully. But when Young had left the storeroom to fetch it, Fred Biggs told Foster that the work was virtually finished. Foster called Young back and told him not to bother. They might as well all go home.

That evening, the Biggses treated themselves to a night out in London on the strength of the overtime money. When he woke up next morning, Fred Biggs felt unwell. He got some pills from his doctor, but was too ill to go to work on the Monday. By Tuesday he had developed chest pains and had difficulty in walking. His feet gave him great pain. That night, he couldn't bear the weight of his bedclothes. He did not sleep. On Thursday 4 November he was admitted to the West Herts Hospital in Hemel Hempstead.

This latest storeroom casualty had Hadland's managing director really worried. There were two rumours circulating among his staff, neither of which he felt he could dismiss any longer. The more popular was that the water supply was in some way contaminated; it had been noticed that all the illnesses followed cups of tea or coffee. The more alarmist theory was that the epidemic had something to do with recent radioactive work on the disused Government airfield adjacent to the factory. Few were any longer convinced by the management's insistence that it was merely a recurrence of a well-known local virus, popularly dubbed 'the Bovingdon bug'. Foster decided he could no longer let the situation drift, and he called in Dr Robert Hynd, Medical Officer of Health for the Hemel Hempstead area, and asked him to investigate.

Graham Young, sole surviving member of the

storeroom staff, was regarded with some suspicion by his workmates – not because he was thought to be behind the illnesses, but because he seemed to have a remarkable immunity. One of the most astute staff members, Diana Smart, went around saying she was convinced he had some kind of infectious disease. Young heard that she was calling him a germ carrier, and later that day Mrs Smart again had a severe attack and was forced to go home. As her illness developed, she began to smell unpleasant, which caused some friction with her husband. Her sex life deteriorated distressingly. At one stage her husband found life with her so intolerable that he walked out; he returned home a week later, when she was largely recovered.

Young was still primarily concerned about the progress of his storeroom colleagues. He kept pestering Foster's secretary for news. On the Friday evening, the day after Biggs had been taken to hospital, he rang Mrs Biggs at home to ask how her husband was. She told him the doctors were unable to pinpoint what was wrong. Young asked if he might visit him, but Mrs Biggs said she would rather he didn't; only family visits were anyway permitted at present. Young telephoned the hospital with the same request, but was puzzled to find that there was no patient there by the name of Fred Biggs. Only later did he discover that this was because Biggs had been transferred to London for specialist attention.

Next day, Young visited his cousin Sandra in St Albans, and told her of the new spate of illnesses.

Things didn't look too good, he told her, for Fred Biggs. When he saw his Aunt Winnie, he told her that his workmate was going blind.

Biggs was in fact examined by seven different doctors during his six days in the Hemel Hempstead hospital, but all could agree on no more than that it was some kind of serious nervous complaint. So on Thursday 11 November, in a much worse condition, he was transferred to the Whittington Hospital in Highgate, London. He continued to deteriorate.

Dr Hynd had meanwhile been acting on Mr Foster's summons. The day that Fred Biggs was moved to London, he visited the plant with a team of doctors including members of the Factory Inspectorate. They made a thorough examination of conditions, but could find no explanation.

Next day, Dr Hynd returned and spoke to the assembled staff. Then he interviewed them all one by one, asking where they lived, whether there had been any local illness, how they themselves had been feeling. Among those who professed to be totally baffled by the epidemic was the storeroom boss, Graham Young.

Meanwhile at the Whittington Hospital, Fred Biggs continued to grow worse and was recorded as being 'very seriously ill, with marked general muscular weakness, but no obvious cause'. The skin on his face and in his scrotum began to grow red and scaly, and then to peel off. He was racked with pain. Like Bob Egle, he could hear what was said to him, but could not reply.

Biggs was transferred again – this time to the

National Hospital for Nervous Diseases in Queen's Square. It was there, at seven a.m. on Friday 19 November, after twenty days of illness, that Fred Biggs died.

When Foster received the news, he dictated a memorandum to be circulated among the Hadland's staff. Graham Young read it in a state of extreme animation, then took it over to Diana Smart. She was desperately upset. Young seemed extremely hot and tense. He told Mrs Smart he couldn't continue with his work, and begged her to help him with the packing he had to do. All he could do was pace up and down.

'Poor old Fred,' he said to her. 'It's terrible. I wonder what went wrong. He shouldn't have died. I was very fond of old Fred.'

The atmosphere at Hadland's was close to panic. Staff knew that the medical authorities had given the plant a clean bill of health; but with Fred Biggs's death there was talk of mediaeval plagues and evil spirits. Several employees announced their intention of quitting. John Hadland, who had by now returned from a lengthy overseas sales trip, desperately called in a local GP, Dr Iain Anderson, who acted as the firm's medical officer, to give the staff a morale-boosting talk.

Anderson came later that same afternoon. The entire work force assembled in the Hadland's canteen, and he began by outlining the three explanations which had been under consideration: radiation poisoning, heavy metal poisoning and a powerful, elusive virus.

The first two had, he said, been ruled out. There was no question of radioactive contamination from the airfield. Heavy metal poisoning had been considered, with especial reference to thallium, which was used industrially in the manufacture of high refractive index lenses such as those made at Hadland's; but a spot check had revealed that no thallium was ever used at the plant.

That left the virus – the Bovingdon Bug. It may seem hard to believe, said Dr Anderson, but that's what it must be. The bug was striking in a particularly vicious and unusual form, and great efforts were being made by medical experts to track down and isolate its causes and effects. He was confident that they would soon come up with the answer. In the meantime, there was no need for undue alarm.

Dr Anderson sat down. Hadland asked if anyone had any questions.

There was a moment's silence, then someone at the back asked rather indignantly why heavy metal poisoning had been ruled out. Weren't the symptoms consistent with those of heavy metal poisoning? The questioner began to go into great detail about the effects of metal poisoning as listed in medical textbooks, and to suggest that the possibility had been too hastily ruled out. It was Graham Young.

Dr Anderson was alarmed. He himself had a private suspicion that heavy metal poisoning could not yet be safely ruled out, and he was trying to play the subject down. He tried to shut the questioner up by repeating the verdicts of the visiting experts. Anderson thought that the staff could only grow more nervous if the subject were pursued. But Young persisted stubbornly in his questions.

'Were the symptoms of those who fell ill different from those of the two men who died?' Young asked. It was a stunning question. Anderson had not considered it, but he at once realized its implications. He replied that there was no reason to suppose so.

'But what about the alopecia[1]?' Young demanded. 'Are you suggesting that alopecia can be psychosomatic?'

Anderson fended off the question. But there was no stopping Young, who launched into an involved diatribe on neurological damage. The doctor looked anxiously across to John Hadland, who declared the meeting closed in as decent haste as possible.

Anderson and Hadland exchanged a glance. Each knew what the other was thinking. Anderson set off after the young storeman who had dominated the meeting. He quickly pinned him down in the storeroom.

He began complimenting Young on his performance, then proceeded to use flattery to get more about himself out of the storeman. Anderson knew well that Young's question about alopecia was both well-informed and up to the minute; the possibility of psychosomatic causation was a vexed medical question which had recently been under discussion in specialist journals.

[1] Loss of hair.

Anderson prodded Young further and further, coming finally to the conclusion that 'he had a very extensive knowledge of one type of poisoning, but in other medical subjects knew very little'.

He went back to talk to John Hadland, who told the doctor that Young had recently been through some sort of mental illness. Both were reluctant to hold this against him, or to use it to jump to any conclusions. They had no idea even which mental hospital Young had been in.

They agreed to give Young the benefit of the doubt for the moment, but both men remained very uneasy after they parted. It was Hadland, however, who took the initiative and decided that something must be done without delay. Unsure of the legal situation, Hadland rang his solicitor to ask if there were any dangers in confiding his suspicions to the police. He had no evidence that anyone had been poisoned, let alone that Graham Young was responsible. It was all so speculative.

Reassured by the lawyer, Hadland rang the police. He spoke to Detective Chief Inspector John Kirkpatrick at Hemel Hempstead police station. Hadland concentrated on outlining the illnesses, and expressing concern that they might be the result of foul play. He was wary of incriminating Young, especially over the phone.

Kirkpatrick went straight up to Bovingdon. He asked to look over the company's employment register, and himself noticed that the start of the sequence of illnesses – the attacks suffered by Egle and Hewitt – coincided with the date of Young's arrival. He wired a selection of employees' names, including Young's, to be checked out in the records at Scotland Yard.

Next day, he tried to contact the head of Hertfordshire CID, Detective Chief Superintendent Ronald Harvey, who was attending a luncheon in London. By an extraordinary coincidence, and one that was to prove most fortunate for Harvey, the lunch was a gathering of forensic scientists. He was called from his table to speak to Kirkpatrick, who gave him the details. Both men were baffled by the symptoms Kirkpatrick outlined; their routine knowledge of the poisons most commonly associated with criminal science suggested nothing. Harvey returned to his seat with a puzzled expression, but could not have been better placed for an answer to his problems. He was sitting between Keith Mant, a forensic pathologist who had worked on police cases with Sir Keith Simpson, and Ian Holden, a former director of the Aldermaston research establishment. When Harvey repeated the symptoms, both men at once diagnosed thallium poisoning. Harvey had never heard of it.

He left the lunch quickly and drove straight to Hemel Hempstead. By now Scotland Yard had replied to Kirkpatrick's list of names with a total blank. Dissatisfied, Kirkpatrick had asked them to recheck on Graham Young.

Anxious to find out more about thallium before coming face to face with a suspect, Harvey was trying to trace a copy of the only book on the subject, Prick's *Thallium Poisoning*, which his lunch companions had recommended, adding that there would be a copy in the library of the Royal Society of Medicine. But it was Saturday, and the RSM was closed; its library books, they were told, were anyway never lent to non-members, not even the police.

A phone call to the police forensic science laboratories revealed that there was another copy at their department in Cheshire. Harvey was told it was the only other copy in the country.[1] He rang Cheshire and demanded the book. It was sent down at once in a squad car, which raced down the M6 and M1 with blue light flashing.

Harvey and Kirkpatrick called Hadland and Foster to county police headquarters near Hatfield to discuss Young. Soon after, Scotland Yard came back with the news that only six months earlier he had been released from Broadmoor, where he had spent nine years for poisoning his sister, his father and a schoolfriend. An officer was sent straight round to Young's digs in Maynards Road.

The Saddiqs were not able to say where Young was; all they knew was that he had gone away for the weekend. Police were despatched to Winifred's home in Leverstock Green, where she was writing Christmas cards when the doorbell rang. She knew her brother was in Sheerness and gave them the address.

A telex message was flashed to Kent constabulary

[1] In fact there was one twenty miles away in the Barbican flat of Professor Francis Camps.

instructing the urgent arrest of Graham Young on suspicion of murder. The officers who went straight round to the address Winifred had given surrounded the house, but found it deserted. A knock at a neighbour's door revealed that they had the wrong house number; Winifred had been so upset by the arrival of the police that she had said ninety-two instead of ninety-three. An acid message was sent back to Harvey, and Kent police tried again.

5

Capable of sustained effort

The Young family had been out for the evening. They were just preparing to go to bed when the doorbell rang. Fred Young answered it. As soon as he saw two police officers on the doorstep, he knew what had happened and why they were there. What he did not know was that his house was entirely surrounded by police in case his son should try to make a break.

'Is Graham Young here?' asked one of the officers.

Fred Young simply stood aside and pointed to his son, who could be seen through the open kitchen door making himself an egg sandwich. The policeman strode straight in and clapped a pair of handcuffs on him; the other began to intone the charge of suspected murder.

Aunt Winnie came into the hall to see what was going on. When she saw the policemen, she said: 'Oh, Graham, what have you done now?'

'I don't know what they're talking about, Auntie.'

Fred Young stood watching in silence. He couldn't speak as Graham was led past him to the police car. He heard his son say 'Which one are you doing me for?' as he got in. Then Fred Young went upstairs to his bedroom, his thoughts going back to his second wife, Molly, whom he was convinced his son had poisoned. He went through all the drawers, taking out every scrap of paper that had anything to do with his son Graham, even his birth certificate. Then he tore them all up into tiny pieces.

Young was taken to Sheerness police station. The officers in charge of him were unable to answer his repeated questions about the charge against him. They knew no more than he did.

At the station, Young was searched and then told to strip. He was given two blankets to wear, and placed in a cell to await the arrival of Detective Chief Inspector Kirkpatrick, who was on his way down from Hemel Hempstead with Detective Sergeant Robert Livingstone.

Livingstone had already been in on a discovery which had shaken everyone at Hemel Hempstead police station. With Detective Inspector John Ratcliffe and Detective Constable Michael Grinstead he had gone back to the semi-detached house in Maynards Road to take a look at Graham Young's bedsitter. All three gasped when they opened the bedroom door.

The walls were festooned with pictures of Hitler and other Nazi leaders, decorated with swastikas. The window sill, tables and shelves were lined with bottles, phials and tubes containing substances of various colours. On a chair just inside the door, the three men saw some crude drawings of grave-yards and tombstones, spidery men clutching their throats, and wielding hypodermic syringes and bottles marked 'Poison'. Many were bald, some were pictured with their hair falling out. There were skulls and crossbones everywhere.

Livingstone rushed back to the station to tell Harvey, and was immediately despatched with Kirkpatrick to Sheerness. Newton and Grinstead began to make a systematic search. They started drawing up an inventory of the bottles and phials, of the drawings and scraps of paper. There were some empty wine bottles and ether bottles in a corner. On the back of a chair hung a brown corduroy jacket in the top pocket of which they found a phial of yellow powder and a scrap of paper with a telephone number on it. It later turned out to be Fred Biggs's.

Under the wardrobe they found a box containing a plastic spoon with traces of white powder in it. The drawer was full of more bottles, some with John Bell and Croyden labels. In the ashtray beside the bed there was an empty phial. On the bedside table there was a pile of books with such titles as *Aids to Forensic Medicine*.

But it was under the bed that Newton made the major discovery. On the floor near the foot of the bed he found a loose-leaf pad described on its cover as A Student's and Officer's Case Book. A quick flick through its closely handwritten pages showed it to be the diary of an expert, calculating and highly intelligent poisoner. Newton took it back straight to Harvey. It was now about three a.m.

Kirkpatrick and Livingstone were approaching Sheerness. They arrived at the police station at three ten. Young was taken from his cell, and at once began his eager questioning. Kirkpatrick told him: 'I am arresting you on suspicion of murder and taking you to Hemel Hempstead police station where further inquiries will be made.'

'Yes, I know,' Young replied. 'But didn't you say murders, plural?'

'No, I did not.'

Young was taken straight to the waiting car without further explanation, still wearing only the blankets. They immediately headed back to Hemel Hempstead.

Young was still eager to know more. 'Is it permitted to ask you one or two questions, Inspector? What are the precise details of the charge against me?'

Kirkpatrick told him that it was not yet settled that he would be charged at all. 'There's a great deal of work to be done,' he said.

'I appreciate that is so in a case such as this. But surely you must supply me with details of the possible charge?'

'You said "a case such as this". What did you mean by that?'

'We won't go into that now. You're bound surely to tell me the name of the person I'm supposed to have murdered?'

'We are making inquiries into the death of your workmate Frederick Biggs, who died on Friday morning.'

'Yes indeed, Inspector, but as far as I know he died of some kind of virus which appears to have

128

affected other people at Hadland's. I shall want to know more than that, Inspector.'

'Well, you tell me what I think you've done.'

'Certainly not, Inspector. As you've told me, it's my entitlement to say nothing, and I'd much rather wait and see what develops. Presuming for a moment I'm guilty of some crime, I'm innocent until proved otherwise. I prefer to wait and see what happens.'

Later, however, Young's arrogance again got the better of him. He began to boast about his perfect crime. He had murdered his stepmother in 1962; she had been declared dead of natural causes, cremated and buried. No-one had suspected a thing.

Kirkpatrick thought it time to try a few questions about Hadland's. He implied that he knew all about Young's activities since he joined the firm in May. Why didn't he make a clean breast of the whole business?

'The whole story is too terrible,' said Young. 'You would be disgusted and amazed.'

Kirkpatrick tried to coax Young by reminding him that two of his victims, Tilson and Batt, were still seriously ill in hospital, and in danger of their lives. Young was more concerned about himself:

'I can't possibly tell you everything, but some things I will. I seemed to be a misfit when I was young. I wasn't like other children. I used to withdraw a lot within myself. I read a lot, and I became obsessed with the macabre. Toxicology has always fascinated me.' Young certainly knew his own press cuttings well.

Kirkpatrick tried to get more out of him about Tilson and Batt. Batt's condition, he told him, was deteriorating. He was suffering from hallucinations.

'That concerns me,' Young broke in, 'as it's obvious the doctors are not treating him properly.'

Kirkpatrick seized his chance: 'What did you poison him with?'

Young thought a moment, then replied: 'I won't tell you the agent I used. But I will tell you what the hospital should give him as an antidote – dymercaprol and potassium chloride.'

Kirkpatrick, noting down the antidote, asked Young to spell it for him.

He got little more out of his suspect. Young boasted that he had mixed Batt's dose himself – a personal recipe – and added that he had used a dissolved powder on the two men who had died. Egle, he said, was given one very large dose, and Biggs three 'fair' doses. Tilson and Batt were each given two smaller liquid doses.

But Young knew well as he talked that he could later deny everything – as indeed he did. He knew too that Kirkpatrick would not be able to make notes of the conversation for some hours, and that this would tell against the officer in court. Both were wary of letting anything slip by pursuing the subject much further. Young repeatedly asked 'Is it only one person I'm accused of killing?'. Kirkpatrick refused to elaborate; he had no licence to do so. Throughout the journey he was amazed by Young's shrewdness, his coolness, and the accuracy of his constant references to the Judge's Rules.

They arrived back in Hemel Hempstead at six thirty-five a.m., by which time Harvey had read the diary, and realized that things were much graver than even he had expected. It mentioned a total of eight supposed victims, each referred to by an initial; Harvey thought he had solved six, all people who had been ill at Hadland's, but he was still baffled by two. He had also had time to look through the book on thallium, hard for a layman to follow because of its highly technical language. He understood enough, however, to know that Jethro Batt and David Tilson, and perhaps others, were in very real danger of dying. He had to see Young at once to find out who else there was, and what could be done for them.

Young was taken straight into Harvey; it was now towards seven a.m. Harvey at once showed him the diary, intimated that he understood all its implications and that he wanted to know more.

'I understand Mr Kirkpatrick has cautioned you?'

'Yes, Detective Chief Superintendent,' Young replied, 'the inspector is conversant with the Judge's Rules and I hope you are.'

Young admitted the diary was his, and that he had written it. Asked who were the people referred to by their initials, he said: 'They are figments of my imagination. I was preparing to write a novel, a work of fiction, and they are my notes.'

Harvey: 'The initials refer to people you worked with at Hadland's, don't they?'

Young: 'Do I have to repeat myself? They are all imaginary.'

131

'Did you give any of these people poison?'

'Absolutely not.'

'Various poisons were found in your room in Maynards Road. Do they belong to you?'

'I expect so. I had poisons there.'

Young became impatient, and began to tell Harvey his business. 'You first have to identify the poisons with which you allege I poisoned people. Then you have to show opportunity. You say I did it. How did I do it? Lastly comes motive. There are three things you have to prove: means, opportunity and motive.'

Harvey in turn became impatient at this, and determined to save Batt, Tilson and whatever others there were. 'Two men have died and two more are seriously ill in hospital. I appeal to you to tell me what poison you administered so that doctors can save them. Some of these people offered you friendship. They tried to help you. Now you have the chance to help them.'

'As you say,' replied Young, 'these people are my friends. So where is the motive? You are trying to trick me.'

Harvey realized he was going to get nothing more out of Young in this mood, so despatched him to a cell for what was left of the night. Young complained about still having nothing but the blankets to wear, and Livingstone was sent home to get some of his son's clothes for him. This established the relationship, common to police grillings, which was to be used against Young during the interviews: Harvey as the hard man, relentlessly driving home questions designed to crack a suspect, Livingstone and (to a lesser extent) Kirkpatrick as the friendly father-figures hoping to win his confidence.

When Harvey confronted Young again at four forty-five on Sunday afternoon, however, there was no need for subtlety. Young was suddenly prepared to talk – again, Harvey realized, because he could not resist boasting about his achievements and about his knowledge of toxicology.

Harvey launched in with deliberate straightness: 'Look,' he said, 'I cautioned you this morning, and that still applies. Now I've been doing some work on your diary and I believe I've identified the people you refer to . . .'

Young broke in: 'May I say something, Inspector – I'm sorry, Superintendent? I do assure you that was a genuine mistake – I like you. You're a forthright man. No sugaring up. You say you've been doing some work. How's it gone? What have you learnt?'

Harvey repeated his belief that he'd identified the initials in the diary. Young knew he was bluffing about some; he must be, for he had no reason to have heard of them. 'Very well, Superintendent,' he said, 'you tell me what you think and I'll tell you if you're right.'

Harvey began to go through the diary date by date, suggesting his own interpretation of the initials.

'B is Bob Egle?'

'Yes.'

'D is David Tilson?'

'Correct.'

'You gave something different to Bob Egle?'

'Yes, I did.'

'Di is Mrs Smart?'

'Yes. What I gave her was something quite different from the others.'

'Is F Fred Biggs?'

'It is.'

'I haven't been able to work out R. Is it Ron Hewitt?'

'No. He did have something, but R did not.'

'In the diary, you say R should visit in the week of 12 October.'

'Yes, he is one of the Ryman drivers. I don't know his name. But he didn't come.'

'You also mention an M and a P.'

'M is Mary Berrows. P is Peter Buck.'

'Are you admitting that you poisoned these people?'

'Yes.'

'Are there any others?'

'I've told you about Ron Hewitt. There was also Peter Buck and Trevor Sparkes – he was with me at the government training centre. I believe he comes from Welwyn Garden City.'

Harvey was shaken. 'I've not previously heard of Sparkes. Is he dead?'

'No. He had several doses, but they were not lethal.'

Harvey proceeded to take Young back to his childhood and the 1962 trial. Young denied nothing, then went on to repeat his boast about getting away with his stepmother's murder. Harvey warned him that he could still be charged with that.[1]

'Anyway,' he told Young, 'what you have admitted amounts to two charges of murder and several of attempted murder.'

'That is an academic point, Superintendent,' Young replied. 'You've got to prove those charges.'

'Very well. You talked last night about means, opportunity and motive. Well, we know the opportunity; you put the poison in their drinks. You've told me the means – thallium and other poisons, which were found in your room. But what about motive? None of these people were your enemies. Why did you do it?'

'I suppose I had ceased to see them as people – or, more correctly, a part of me had. They became guinea pigs.'

Harvey turned to the bizarre list Newton had brought back from Young's bedsitter.

The ether? 'I used to inhale it. I am not addicted to it, though. Ether is not addictive. Its effects are similar to those of alcohol.'

The graveyard sketch? 'A rather macabre drawing I did under the influence of ether.'

A bottle containing sodium tartrate mixed with antimony salt: 'I used it on Di Smart.' The bottles containing thallium: 'I used it on Bob Egle and Fred Biggs, then on Jethro Batt and David Tilson.' The

---

[1]Harvey was bluffing, for he well knew that this was not so, as no reference to Young's previous offences could be made if he pleaded not guilty to these new ones.

135

bottles containing antimony potassium tartrate: 'I used it on Peter Buck, Di Smart, Ron Hewitt and Trevor Sparkes.'

The phial found in his jacket breast-pocket, containing thallium: 'It was my exit dose. But I didn't have a chance to use it. I had not anticipated being arrested in Sheerness.'

He volunteered the information that he had obtained the thallium and other poisons from the London chemists, plus another in St Albans saying he had wanted them for 'qualitative and quantitative analysis.'

Harvey knew he could draw Young out if he flattered his scientific know-how. 'What fascinates me,' he said, 'is your expertise with poisons. You must have studied a great deal to have so extensive knowledge.'

'Very little, in fact, since I was fourteen,' Young replied. 'I have not had the opportunity.' They both knew why. 'But I am fortunate in having a most retentive memory.'

Harvey pursued the technical discussion of the poisons Young had used, and asked him about the dosages allotted to each victim. Why had he chosen thallium for some, and antimony for others?

'Antimony is less toxic, and is more rapidly eliminated from the system. I prefer not to tell you how I selected who should have which poison.'

But Young was warming to his subject. He asked Harvey if he would like a complete run-down on the nature and effects of thallium. Harvey nodded, and Young launched into a twenty-minute lecture:

'Thallium is still a relatively unused poison in this country, employed in the manufacture of certain types of highly refractory optical glasses. It is no longer used as a rodenticide, but has been used in tests for tuberculosis . . .

'After ingestion of a fatal dose, death would be inevitable unless a strong emetic was taken within thirty minutes. Some hours later a person might vomit, but by then it would be too late . . .

'There would be diarrhoea and pain. Then a loss of sensation in the extremities of the toes and fingers, extending to all limbs, caused by the poison breaking down the tissue of the nerves . . .'

Young went on to speak of the effects on the respiratory system, the eyes and the brain, until death ensued. Thallium is an accumulative poison, he said, which causes death if sufficient small doses, themselves not necessarily fatal, were administered over a consistent period. The symptoms displayed by the victim are loss of hair, soreness and scaliness of the skin, stomach pains, sickness, diarrhoea, lines on the fingernails known as Mees lines, degeneration of the nerve fibres, loss of control of the limbs culminating in paralysis and delirium, often suicidal, with hallucinations. He compared its effects with the less severe consequences of antimony poisoning, which leads to similar vomiting, diarrhoea and stomach pains, but is rarely fatal. It is sometimes used as an emetic.

Harvey had stopped taking notes. The description was full of medical terms which meant nothing to him. One passage from the diary kept going through his mind as Young flowed on: 'There are few doctors in this country who can identify thallium poisoning.'

Young stopped talking. Harvey looked up, and Young said: 'You must feel revulsion for me.'

Harvey said simply: 'Do you know what the things you have described mean in human terms?'

'Not completely,' Young replied. 'I have never seen death.'

There was a moment's silence. Then Harvey said: 'This evidence is not conclusive. Will you make a written statement?'

Young laughed. Harvey was to remember this later as the only moment he ever saw Young show any humour at all. 'No,' said Young. Then: 'If I did, I could always say it was taken under duress.'

'That's up to you. Will you make a statement?'

'I don't know.' Young thought a moment. 'You seem a fair man, Superintendent. I'll sleep on it, and let you know tomorrow.'

By tomorrow, Harvey hoped, he would have the conclusive evidence he needed. As he sent Young back to his cell, he knew that his next appointment was at St Pancras Hospital at two thirty the following afternoon for the post-mortem on Frederick Biggs.

Professor Hugh Molesworth-Johnson, senior lecturer in forensic medicine at St Thomas' Hospital Medical School, had spent all weekend mugging up on his knowledge of thallium after receiving a call from Harvey asking for an urgent post-mortem. He had consulted the professor of medicine at the University of Ghent, Belgium, an acknowledged international expert, who had dealt with an outbreak of thallium poisoning in the Low Countries in the 1950s. He asked Professor John Cavanagh, neuropathologist at the London Institute of Neurology, to be present. They met Harvey and his officers at the hospital; also present were a police photographer and Mr Nigel Fuller of the Metropolitan Police Forensic Science Laboratory.

Harvey virtually leant over Molesworth-Johnson's shoulder as the post-mortem progressed. All present knew exactly what they were looking for. The pathologist found that the face had suffered purple-brownish discoloration. The skin around the nose was red and scaly, and breaking away in places. The same had happened in the scrotum. The hair of Biggs's head could be pulled out astonishingly easily; as Molesworth-Johnson said later, 'It came away in great wads'. There was, however, no baldness. There were noticeable changes of pigmentation. All these signs constituted symptoms of thallium poisoning, as did the reddening of the air passages which indicated the onset of pneumonia. But the characteristic Mees lines on the nails had not developed. And, as hard as he looked, Molesworth-Johnson could not find any trace at all of thallium.

He conducted a microscopic examination of the internal organs, and concluded that Biggs had been a healthy man until this terminal illness. He presumed that Biggs had not been ill long enough for more marked symptoms of thallium poisoning to develop. Professor Cavanagh examined sections of the brain, the spinal cord and other nerves. But neither man could find traces of the poison itself. Molesworth-Johnson had to record on the post-mortem certificate: 'Cause of death not established.' He prepared the organs to be handed over to Fuller for scientific examination. The proof of thallium poisoning was not in fact to be established until some days later, when Fuller analysed Biggs's organs at the police laboratories.

Nevertheless, Harvey hurried back to Hemel Hempstead – minus the evidence he had hoped for – with one intent in mind. At ten p.m. he charged Graham Young with the murder of Frederick Biggs. 'I have no wish to say anything' was Young's response. The police still had no proof at all that Biggs had died from poisoning.

Harvey and Young next met at one ten p.m. next day, Tuesday 23 November. Young was in un-characteristically penitent mood. Harvey gave him a cigarette. 'Have you slept well?' he asked him. 'Well, thank you,' Young replied.

'Do you', he asked the superintendent, 'know the *Ballad of Reading Gaol*?' Harvey said he remembered it from his schooldays, but not in any detail. Young began to recite a verse:

> Yet each man kills the thing he loves,
>   By each let this be heard.
> Some do it with a bitter look,
>   Some with a flattering word.
> The coward does it with a kiss,
>   The brave man with a sword.

'I suppose,' said Young, 'I could be said to kiss.'

There was a moment's silence, then he added: 'You've treated me much better than I deserve.'

Harvey turned to Kirkpatrick: 'I think he's beginning to feel some remorse.' It was the first sign of this he had noticed. But Young quickly contradicted him: 'No, Mr Harvey. That would be hypocritical. What I feel is in the emptiness of my soul.'

Harvey suggested that Young went back to his cell. There was work to be done.

'Yes,' said Young. 'It's over. The charade is over.'

Earlier that day, Young had made a brief appearance at Hemel Hempstead Magistrates' Court, where he had been charged with the murder of Frederick Biggs, and remanded in custody by the chairman of the bench, Mr Lewis Dean. Police had secured him a local solicitor, Mr John Pickworth. It was decided to hold Young for a few more days in a cell at Hemel Hempstead until further charges against him could be settled.

It was just as well Harvey felt able to bring the charge against Young as soon as he did. The local evening paper, the Thomson-owned *Evening Echo*, had by now discovered that all was not well in Bovingdon, and was putting out speculative stories on the basis of interviews with Hadland's staff. Reporters had heard of the suspicious death of Frederick Biggs, well-known in the area as a local councillor, and were now told that it had been preceded four months before by that of Bob Egle. The paper led on scare stories about radioactive contamination from the adjacent airfield – itself

141

much in the news in recent months because of a controversial plan to build a prison there. Young was in court before the *Echo* had even established that it was a murder inquiry.

Harvey's next move was to apply to the coroner at Gillingham, Norfolk, for permission to exhume the ashes of Robert Egle, buried there after his cremation at Amersham. Gillingham had been Egle's home town, and his widow had moved down there to live with a sister after his death. The coroner duly reopened the inquest on Egle, and had the ashes exhumed. They were sent, as Biggs's organs had been, to Nigel Fuller at the Metropolitan Police Forensic Science Laboratories for analysis.

It took Fuller ten days to come up with the evidence Harvey needed: Biggs and Egle had both died of thallium poisoning. In the case of Biggs, Fuller found 120 micrograms of thallium per gram in the gut, twenty micrograms per gram in the left kidney, five in muscle samples, five in bone matter samples and ten in brain matter. He found the largest quantities in the large intestine and kidneys. He also recorded that the roots of Biggs's head and pubic hairs had turned black – another symptom of thallium poisoning. He found six micrograms of thallium per millilitre in a sample of Bigg's urine. Fuller calculated that all these amounts would have been considerably larger when first ingested – more than enough to ensure inevitable death.

When analysing Egle's ashes, Fuller found a total of nine milligrams of thallium in a total weight of

1,780 grams of ash. He calculated that this would have been equivalent to about five micrograms per gram before cremation had burnt off most of the poison's remaining traces. To ensure that his conclusions were scientifically watertight, Fuller also examined the cremated remains of another man, to see if he could find any trace at all of thallium; he knew that it was possible for any human being to ingest tiny amounts of thallium from the atmosphere during his or her lifetime. The examination of the second set of ashes revealed no thallium at all. Fuller had conclusive scientific evidence that Egle's death had been quite wrongly diagnosed; he had died of thallium poisoning.

On 3 December, Young was charged with Egle's murder. It was the first time in criminal history that a murder charge had followed the exhumation of cremated ashes.

To avoid any shadow of doubt, Fuller also analysed a kidney of Egle's which had been mounted and preserved at St Albans City Hospital because of the unusual nature of his decline and death. Allowing for the tenfold reduction in quantities caused by mounting the organ, Fuller found the equivalent of 2.5 micrograms per gram of thallium. At Harvey's instigation, he also analysed urine and hair samples from Tilson and Batt. Batt's hair proved under the microscope to have blackened at the roots, while Tilson's had not. Fuller went on to examine blood and urine samples from Smart, Buck and Sparkes, but found no traces at all of thallium.

Finally, Fuller examined earth samples from Biggs's garden, plus all his garden equipment, in case Young were to assert that he had absorbed the thallium accidentally from physical contact with it as an insecticide. Fuller found nothing. From re-examination of the organs, however, he concluded that Biggs must have ingested some hundreds of grams of thallium. He knew that one gram would be a certainly fatal dose. A level teaspoon of thallium weighs more than ten grams.

It was also Fuller who undertook the more routine work of establishing the nature of all the chemicals and powders found in Young's room. The phial in the top pocket of his corduroy jacket, Young's self-styled 'exit dose', contained 2.24 grams of thallium acetate, more than twice the fatal dose. Another sample tube contained 17.81 milligrams of thallium acetate, another 415 milligrams of aspirin with traces of thallium. The bottle with the John Bell and Croyden label, found beside the bed, contained 32.33 grams of antimony sodium tartrate – more than 200 times a fatal dose. It was this antimony that Young had fed to all his victims except Egle, Biggs, Batt and Tilson. Next day he was formally charged by Harvey with causing grievous bodily harm to Diana Smart, Peter Buck, Ronald Hewitt and Trevor Sparkes, by the administration of poison.

These charges were added to the list at Young's next weekly court appearance. He had by now been transferred to Brixton Prison, where he was kept in the sick wing, because of the threat he posed other prisoners and remandees.

In April, when he had been in Brixton for four months, Young was one day approached by another inmate, who asked for a private word with him. Carlton, as Young remembered his name, said he had heard about thallium, knew something of its properties, and was anxious to know more. He also wished to know where and how he could get hold of some. Would Young tell him? Young did not commit himself. Then Carlton asked him to prepare a document containing as much as he could tell him about thallium. Young suspected it was a put-up job, that Carlton had been enlisted by the police to extract from him a document which could be used in court. 'To me the whole thing stank. I was sure it was a police set-up. I decided to play along with the idea, and see if it was used in court,' Young explained when in fact it was. The document had found its way into Harvey's hands, and had come up in his evidence, but little had been made of it. 'I now see', Young admitted, 'that this was a spontaneous gesture on Carlton's part, so that his barrister could turn round at his trial and say "Well, there you are, this man has done invaluable service in this other case etc".' The incident was never again mentioned.

Young received regular visits from his solicitor, John Pickworth, while in Brixton, and was undismayed when he was told that the police had built up a formidable case against him. He had every intention of challenging all the medical evidence. When he appeared at Hemel Hempstead Magistrates' Court on 22 March to be committed for trial,

Young stood in the dock quite unmoved as the now familiar charges were again rehearsed, and the names of seventy-five witnesses – more than half of them doctors – were read out by the prosecution, and bound over by the magistrate to attend his trial at St Albans Crown Court. An attempt was made by the prosecution to have the witnesses bound over without their names being read out in open court, but the presiding magistrate, again Mr Lewis Dean, overruled the Director of Public Prosecutions' representative, and insisted they be read in full. This was the first indication that the Home Office was to be extremely sensitive about the Young case, and to do everything in its power to prevent press or public pursuing detailed inquiries in the normal way.

Back in Brixton, Young was adamant about pleading not guilty to all charges when brought to trial. He was not going to make the same mistake he had made in 1962; by accepting legal advice then, and pleading guilty, he had found his trial all over in ten minutes, and had won a mere modicum of the publicity and public prominence he had hoped for. By now as much a legal as a scientific old hand, Young knew well the strength of his position. With six charges, seventy-five potential witnesses and a blanket plea of not guilty, he could be sure of a long drawn out trial with the maximum of front-page publicity – not least when the only defence witness, Graham Young, took the stand.

His obstinacy soon had Pickworth at his wits' end. He approached several distinguished QCs, but had great difficulty in finding one who could take on the case; and the trial, originally scheduled for May, had to be postponed. The new and inadequately equipped courthouse at St Albans – only recently elevated to the status of Hertfordshire's Crown Court with the abolition of Assizes and Quarter-Sessions – was also having its own problems at the prospect of staging so major a trial. Another judge had to be laid on to ensure the minimum of delay to the court's already heavy schedule.

After a further postponement, a date was finally fixed; the trial would open on 19 July. Mr Justice Eveleigh would preside. Eveleigh, aged fifty-four, had been Recorder of Burton-on-Trent and Gloucester before becoming a High Court judge in 1968; renowned as one of Britain's severest judges, he was one of the few still to carry his black cap at murder trials. With only days to spare, Pickworth managed to retain the services of Sir Arthur Irvine, QC, Solicitor-General for the last three years of the Wilson Government, to defend Young, with Mr Freddie Beazely as his junior. The press, who had begun to unearth Young's past, and sensed what embarrassment the trial's end and its revelations would cause the Government, prepared to give the Young murder trial major front-page coverage.

Young waited in Brixton, finding boredom his biggest enemy. 'I attempt to circumvent it by reading or playing chess against myself,' he wrote to his sister. 'The latter is a somewhat schizophrenic exercise, calling for almost superhuman detachment, but at least I have the consolation that I invariably win!

At present I exist in a sort of limbo, my remands having finished and my trial yet to come. I can imagine how anxious you are to see the whole thing finished with. I, too, wish to see the end of this unfortunate episode. I trust that it will end in victory – the alternative would be the finish of me.' He had written to her in an earlier letter: 'I do not know what you have been told of this affair, but it appears that the family have already tried and judged it. I need hardly add that this is a trifle distressing.'

To his cousin Sandra, Young wrote: 'Why is no-one replying to my letters? Perhaps they were discouraged by my grim attempts at humour. Honestly, though, I see little purpose in writing sepulchral, doom-laden epistles to them.' He referred to his boredom in prison, saying: 'At least it gives me the opportunity to reflect upon the past and to plan for the future. One of the things I miss most in here is my intermittent sessions in the arms of Bacchus! As you can imagine, the prison is dry, and no alcohol has passed my lips for many a month. I have been transformed into an abstemious person, fit to grace the board of a temperance society!'

The letter ended: 'I stand a good chance of acquittal, for the prosecution case has a number of inherent weaknesses. A strong point in my favour is that I am NOT guilty of the charges against me – antecedents notwithstanding. My trial will, I hope, vindicate me.'

6

Of above average intelligence

The St Albans trial got off to a bad start. Young, arraigned and charged, visibly revelled in the curiosity of the public gallery above him as he stood between the dock's bulletproof screens. The names of the all-male jury were called out, and no objection entered by either side. Then the clerk of the court rose for the swearing-in procedure, and read them the wrong oath. 'We'd better start again,' muttered Mr Justice Eveleigh. There was uneasy laughter in court.

Graham Young had pleaded not guilty to ten charges, two of them alternatives. There was the murder of Robert Egle on or about 7 July, 1971, and of Frederick Biggs on or about 19 November; the attempted murder of David Tilson on or about 8 October, and of Jethro Batt on 15 October; and on various dates between 8 February and 21 October the malicious administration of poison, with intent to cause grievous bodily harm, to Trevor Sparkes, Ronald Hewitt, Peter Buck and Diana Smart. The same charge was also preferred with respect to

149

Tilson and Batt as an alternative to the attempted murder charge.[1]

The most macabre episode of Young's trial, with the exception of his own two-day appearance in the dock, came at once that first morning when Mr John Leonard QC, having outlined the prosecution case, spent twenty minutes reading almost the entire text of the diary found beneath Young's bed. Inevitably labelled the 'diary of death' by the popular press, it is a unique chronicle of a murderer's day-to-day activities, methodical, impassive and self-important.

The diary contained entries for 12, 13, 14 and 18 October; then some pages had been torn out; the entries continued with 21 and 31 October, then 1, 3, 4, 10, 16 and 17 November. It was written by hand on the loose-leaf pages in blue ink. All the victims were referred to by the initials which had caused Harvey such difficulty.

F stood for Fred Biggs. 31 October: 'I have administered a fatal dose of the special compound to F, and anticipate a report on his progress on Monday 1 November. I gave him three separate doses.' 1 November: 'F was not at work today.' 3 November: 'News from other fronts . . . F is now seriously ill. He is unconscious, and has developed paralysis and blindness. It is likely that he will decline in the next few days. It will be a merciful release for him, as if he should survive he will be permanently impaired.

---

[1]The murder and attempted murder charges applied to those victims poisoned with thallium, the lesser charges to those allegedly poisoned with antimony.

Even if the blindness is reversed, organic brain disease would render him a husk. It is better that he should die. From my point of view his death would be a relief. It would remove one more casualty from what is rapidly becoming a crowded field of battle.'
4 November: 'A doctor has said the illness of F is due to a virus, and that there is a lot of it going around. Is someone setting up in opposition to me?'
10 November: 'F must have phenomenal strength to fight the special compound. If he lives it could be inconvenient. Too many health authorities are becoming involved for me to press the matter further.' 17 November: 'The latest news from the hospital is that F is responding to treatment. He is being obstinately difficult. If he survives a third week he will live. That could be inconvenient. I am most annoyed. He is surviving far too long for my peace of mind.' This was the last entry concerning Biggs, who died three days later. Young, who claimed the diary was all written on one evening[1], 18 November, clearly didn't have time or opportunity to finish it.

J referred to Jethro Batt. 18 October: 'A second development, and one which I now regret, is that J has been afflicted.' 21 October: 'I feel rather ashamed of my action in harming J. I think he is a really nice fellow, and the nearest to a friend that I have at Hadland's. I have faith he will recover.' 4 November: 'J's condition remains unchanged. The

---

[1]Inaccuracies in some of his dating would seem to support this.

doctor has concluded that his illness is due to a virus.'

In the case of D – David Tilson – the diary outlined a plan to visit him in hospital and 'pretend to commiserate by offering him a miniature bottle of brandy', then to get him to drink it immediately so the nurses would not discover it. Then a second visit was to follow, but this time the brandy would be doctored. 'This would bring a deterioration in D's condition within a week and would end in death.' It was 'the perfect opportunity for a protracted study'. But the plan was thwarted. 'D has not been hospitalized – happy for him – and therefore is free to live out his allotted span. For needless to say it would be injudicious of me to focus my attention on him for a second time. I don't expect to see him for some time.' Tilson's condition did, however, deteriorate, and he was again admitted to hospital. 1 November: 'A disturbing symptom has occurred. D has started losing hair.' 3 November: 'D's loss of hair is almost total. The hospital feels it might be due to poison. I must watch the situation very carefully. If it looks like I will be detected then I shall have to destroy myself. The events of the next few days will prove decisive. They will point either to my continuation to live or my destruction by my own hand. If I were detected, I would have to follow the maxim: "Those who live by the sword die by the sword".' But as Young told police after his arrest, he never had a chance to use his 'exit dose'.

The only malice shown in the diary occurs in the entry about Diana Smart, referring to the day she told staff she thought Young must be a germ carrier. 'Di irritated me intensely yesterday, so I packed her off home with an attack of illness. I only gave her something to shake her up. I now regret I didn't give her a larger dose, capable of laying her up for a few days.'

An extract revealing the breadth of Young's plans referred to R, whom Harvey had thought to be Ron Hewitt, but who was in fact a driver for Ryman's, the stationery firm, who delivered to the Bovingdon plant regularly. 'R is an ideal subject. He should visit this week and the chance will appear then. This time I must restrain my tendency to over-liberal doses. In a way it seems a shame to condemn such a likeable man to such a horrible end, but I have made my decision and therefore he is doomed to premature decease.' As it was, Ryman's did not deliver that week.

During his appearance in the dock, Young claimed that the diary was a work of fiction. 'I am interested in developing my somewhat stilted style as a narrative writer,' he said. 'The diary was an attempt to elaborate a theory that there was someone with homicidal tendencies in the storeroom at Hadland's. It was purely the expression of a theory, a somewhat fanciful one, which I outlined for my own amusement – though that is not a particularly apt word.'

Young only agreed to refer to the diary as a diary 'under protest – for the sake of convenience'. In fact, he explained, it was 'not a diary at all. It is set out in diary form, but it is not a number of entries set out over a period of days or weeks. It is a document which was completed on one occasion.'

He went on: 'The illnesses were unusual in origin and many of us were naturally concerned to know their cause. A number of things sprang to mind, one being virus infection. Something that also sprang to mind – well, to my mind, at any rate – was the similarity of symptoms displayed by people at the firm and the symptoms of heavy metal poisoning. In consequence I decided to elaborate my theory and suggest circumstances under which these things could have come about. I intended to elaborate it in the form of a short story or novel, for this was not something I seriously believed. I did at first attempt to set it out in the form of a novel, but my style of writing is somewhat stilted. In consequence, I tore out the first one or two leaves.'

Young said that writing was 'something I have always dabbled in'. He had in the past submitted stories about both world wars to an English teacher 'for critical analysis'. He had also submitted a short story to *Reader's Digest* – 'I never heard any more about it, but at least I submitted it'. The authors he most admired were Dennis Wheatley and Bram Stoker, creator of Dracula.

Asked about the opening line of the diary – 'My fears prove to be unfounded' – Young said he had had to invent a fictional character with homicidal tendencies to elaborate his theory. 'From my point of view it had to be fictional that these illnesses could have come about as a result of heavy metal intoxication. They would hardly have been due to multiple accidental dosages or multiple suicidal dosages.' Mr Justice Eveleigh intervened to ask: 'Are you saying that you conjectured a metallic poison as the cause of these illnesses?' Young replied: 'Yes, that is so, my Lord. Conjecture is a better word than fiction. I am much obliged.'

The coolness, the arch phraseology, the officialese and legal jargon, the brazen total denial – contriving even an air of aggrieved innocence – were characteristic of Young's two-day performance in the dock. And a calculated performance it was: neat black suit, immaculate grooming, one hand generally in his left trouser pocket, the other resting on the bar rail, the refusal to sit, the occasional sips of water, the requests for adjournments to gather his thoughts – all combined to produce the impressive histrionic performance designed to earn him the publicity he coveted. Throughout the trial Young studied the press reports with great interest. He personally asked Harvey to issue a photograph to the press, who had been clamouring for one; Young himself specified which one should be released. The *Sun* caused a journalistic rumpus by breaking the embargo on the picture, which soon became famous and accompanied all press reports of Young's crimes. Young took it himself as a passport photograph in an automatic booth on Victoria Station. It has been said to epitomize the frightening face of a killer, with its aggressive stare, its piercing eyes. In fact Young, like many people using those machines, had been deceived by the long delay between the insertion of the coin and the flash of the first photograph; he was leaning forward angrily to bang the machine with his fist when the light flashed and the pose he longed for was inadvertently immortalized. Young was very pleased with it. Once the picture began appearing in the press, he kept asking his warders if Madame Tussauds had yet applied for the details necessary to accord him a place in their Chamber of Horrors, alongside his hero William Palmer.

Leonard made no attempt to explain motive. Despite one or two useful pieces of evidence – Young's irritation with Di Smart, his displeasure at Fred Biggs's unwanted advice – it was clear that Young's victims were simply scientific guinea-pigs, the nearest raw material for chemical experiment. There was even no real distinction between those who died and those who survived. Some victims were used for thallium experiments, some for antimony; the deaths of Egle and Biggs simply confirmed the success or failure of a particular dosage, depending upon the terms of Young's experiment.

For his part, Young denied everything. He challenged all the medical evidence. He made out that his admitted interest in poisons and chemicals was being speciously used to incriminate him. 'I have a tendency to stockpile,' he said to explain the poison horde found in his bedsitter. 'I don't believe that the fact that a person stockpiles dangerous poisons means he is going to use them against people.' Repeatedly confronted by the prosecution with the sequence of illnesses at Hadland's, Young simply shrugged his shoulders and referred to 'our old friend the Bovingdon bug'.

He then began to elaborate an explanation of the partial confession he had made to Harvey under questioning. Young claimed he had made a bargain with the officers that he would provide a 'plausible set of answers' if they would give him food, sleep, access to a solicitor, and clothes. Still in the blankets which he had worn since his arrest in Kent, he had felt, he said, 'like a Sioux Indian'. Young tried to maintain that he had been confident his 'fake confession' would be proved impossible by forensic evidence. This gave John Leonard his first chance to try to puncture Young's self-confidence with some highly aggressive questioning.

'Are you seriously suggesting that a police officer of senior standing was prepared to make a deal with a man charged with murder to accept merely plausible answers on which to base his case?'

'I can only repeat that I thought my statement would be proved wrong.'

'You are an intelligent person. Are you really saying you were prepared to confess in these circumstances merely to get your material comforts? Wasn't that a considerable risk?'

'I chose the two poisons I knew were in my room because I wanted the confession to be convincing.'

Young was unshaken. 'Though this revelation may take you aback, Mr Leonard, if I give my word I tend to keep it.'

Young's blandness rattled Leonard, and the examination soon became an extraordinary battle of wits which provided those present with a powerful glimpse of Young's capacities. Leonard recalled Harvey's evidence that Young had been arrogant throughout his police grillings, and said: 'If I may say so, Mr Young, you display during the course of your evidence a remarkable calmness.'

'I do not feel particularly calm, Mr Leonard, but I am not a person who manifests a great amount of emotion.'

Young soon sensed Leonard's tactic and began to play down the arrogance which clearly would not endear him to the jury. When Leonard recalled Young's cockiness in telling police the antidote doctors should be using on Tilson and Batt, Young was ready to take him on at his own game.

'Do you honestly believe, Mr Young, that the doctors needed your advice? You do by your own admission have an extensive knowledge of toxicology, but did you really know more about these things than the hospital doctors?'

'No. I assumed they would already have commenced this treatment. It would have been highly presumptuous of me to tell a hospital what treatment should be given.'

As the exchanges grew more and more acid, they were clearly building to some kind of climax. For much of the time, as Leonard remorselessly went over and over the ground, Young easily held his own. On Fred Biggs's death:

Leonard: 'Were you so concerned about what happened that you were unable to do any work that day? You knew you had just killed a second man.'

Young: 'That is not so. From the picture you paint of me, you would have thought that I would have been gleefully rejoicing.'

Leonard: 'Your expressions of regret at Mr Biggs's death were pure hypocrisy. His death satisfied you.'

Young: 'No. I can see very little satisfaction to be derived from the death of a man in circumstances like that.'

Leonard: 'Neither can I, Mr Young.'

This kind of point-scoring continued as Young explained that he had given a false name when purchasing poisons because 'to obtain a Schedule One poison the prospective purchaser has to complete a form under Section 11 of the Dangerous Poisons Act. This has to be countersigned by a householder to the effect that the purchaser is of good character, and it has also to be signed by the local police. As you can imagine, this is a time-consuming and somewhat tiresome procedure so I decided to take a short cut.' He had used the pseudonym of Evans so as not to be involved in 'an embarrassing dispute' if he was found out.

'You may think this irresponsible, Mr Leonard, and I may agree; but it was hardly felonious.'

'I suggest you knew perfectly well you were buying those poisons for use on human beings.'

'That is not so. I performed various tests on the thallium I bought to establish its solubility, and its compatibility or incompatibility with other chemicals.'

Pressed by Leonard, Young agreed that he had not

had the necessary equipment for full tests, but said he had done 'as much as I could'. He had further tested thallium's power as an insecticide 'on wayside weeds'.

Leonard: 'You administered the thallium to four people, killing two of them and seriously harming two others.'

Young: 'I administered thallium to no-one. I performed the tests to satisfy my own curiosity about certain chemical problems. To some extent, one might say that my interest in these substances was that of a collector.'

Questioned about the phial of thallium found in his jacket pocket and described as his 'exit dose', Young said he did not think it of great significance. 'Had I wished to commit suicide, Mr Leonard, I had other agents available which would have killed me in a far shorter space of time.'

Leonard gained some ground by displaying the horrific drawings found in Young's room. He passed them to the jury for close examination, then held them aloft for the entire court to see. 'They have the classic look of shock for a horror comic,' said Leonard. 'The figures written on them correspond exactly to the fatal doses of thallium involved in this case.'

'They are a symbolic representation of scenes from my novel,' replied Young. 'The baldness is not significant. They are clearly gross distortions. The faces could be expressing aggression as much as shock.'

Rediscussion of the diary maintained a similar

160

stalemate. Leonard: 'As a work of fiction it jumps into the middle of the story pretty quickly, doesn't it?'

Young: 'Yes, but diaries often do.'

Leonard: 'Did you intend the diary for publication?'

Young: 'No, I had no intention of pushing it for publication. As I have said, I was writing for my own amusement.'

Leonard: 'You have great confidence, Mr Young, in your ability to escape detection in the first place, and in the second place to escape conviction.'

Young: 'That is your opinion, Mr Leonard. You can hardly expect me to agree with it.'

When the climax of the contest came, it was Young who decidedly came off the winner. Leonard was referring to the passage in the diary which mentions the further sequence of unexplained illnesses and comments: 'Is someone setting up in opposition to me?' The question mark was followed by three exclamation marks.

'Isn't that, Mr Young, a rather flippant remark in what is purported to be the serious journal of a fictitious poisoner?'

'Since when, Mr Leonard, have poisoners been noted for their absence of humour?'

'I don't know, Mr Young. I've never met any.'

(With a courteous bow) 'Thank you, Mr Leonard.'

(Flustered) 'You appreciate, Mr Young, that this trial is not yet concluded.'

Young's counsel, Sir Arthur Irvine, expressed the grudging admiration felt by all when discussing

Young's performance during his summing-up: 'He was not unimpressive, was he?'

Sir Arthur clearly felt, as did Leonard, that there was no need for a summing-up speech of any great proportions. Both spoke for under an hour. Sir Arthur repeatedly apologized for questioning police evidence, stressing that he was only doing his job. Then he briefly presented Young's stonewall defence as convincingly as was possible, recalling Young's perpetual insistence on showing off his medical knowledge, and asking if this would be the natural practice of a man trying to conceal murder. Referring to the interview with Dr Anderson which was his final undoing, Sir Arthur asked: 'Would it not be a most extraordinary thing in the atmosphere of that meeting for a guilty man to reveal and parade his knowledge of the subject? He is a zealot on the theme.'

The jury took barely an hour over their verdicts, most of it sorting out the complexities of the alternative charges. While they were out, Young told his warders down in the cells that when sentence was pronounced he would commit suicide by breaking his own neck on the rail of the dock. When he returned for the verdicts, therefore, he had a double guard of four men to restrain him. In fact he took the verdicts and sentences totally impassively, and was the first to turn after Mr Justice Eveleigh had finished speaking.

The jury found Young guilty of the murders of Egle and Biggs; guilty of attempting to murder Batt and Tilson; and guilty of administering poison to

Hewitt and Mrs Smart. They acquitted him of administering poison to Sparkes and Buck because the evidence was not sufficiently clear. The alternative charges referring to Batt and Tilson were dropped.

Sir Arthur Irvine then rose to reveal where Young had been during those nine years which had been so conspicuously skirted over throughout the trial. There were few people in court who did not know it. But the press had given the trial generous space throughout its ten days so they could capitalize on this moment in fine style. The BBC thought the news of sufficient moment to interrupt afternoon music programmes with newsflash announcements.

'In considering sentence,' said Sir Arthur, 'I submit that your Lordship should bear in mind one matter which I mention with the greatest reluctance. I refer to it in my duty, as I conceive it to be, to my client Graham Young. It is that it was possible for Graham Young to commit these offences only because he had been released on licence from Broadmoor.

'This release may appear to have been a serious error of judgement, but the authorities had a duty to protect Young from himself as well as a duty to protect the public.

'If your Lordship is balancing the desirability of a custodial sentence with that of a hospital order, I think it is right that I should say to your Lordship that Young himself thinks that the prison sentence would be better for his condition than a return to Broadmoor.'

Graham Young smiled. He had not only stage-managed the trial which had won him the notoriety he had always coveted, he had even managed to sentence himself.

Sir Arthur concluded: 'The Broadmoor experience thus far has had the tragic consequences of which we have learned in this trial. Your Lordship may think a prison sentence is preferable.' Harvey gave the court details of Young's 1962 offences and of his Broadmoor sentence.

Mr Justice Eveleigh sentenced Young to life imprisonment for the two counts of murder and the two of attempted murder; for administering poison to Hewitt and Mrs Smart he sentenced him to five years' imprisonment on each count, to run consecutively but concurrently with the life sentence.

The foreman of the jury then rose to ask the judge if he could make a statement on the jury's behalf. Mr Eveleigh replied: 'In the circumstances, that would be highly undesirable.' But when the foreman said the statement was about the sale of poisons, the judge agreed. The foreman then read a prepared statement: 'The members of the jury in this case consider it to be our duty to draw the attention of the authorities concerned to the failings of the present system by which poisons are sold to the public. We urge that the system be reviewed in order that in future the public may be more consistently safeguarded.' The judge then thanked the jury for their close attention in 'this nasty case'.

Young's family were allowed ten minutes with him in the cells. His sister's account of the meeting described him as seeming 'genuinely upset'. He sent his regards to Harvey, saying that there were 'no hard feelings', and to Winifred's dog. He apologized to his Aunt Winnie, who was in tears. Then he was taken away to Wormwood Scrubs, from where he was later transferred to Parkhurst maximum security prison on the Isle of Wight.

7

Drawing no attention to himself

The Home Secretary, Reginald Maudling, was on his feet in the House of Commons within an hour of the verdict. 'The Secretary of State for Social Services [Sir Keith Joseph] and I,' he said, 'immediately we learnt of this case, instituted a searching examination of the arrangements for discharging and supervising restricted patients. This is an area raising issues of profound difficulty.'

It had in fact been a hectic twenty-four hours for Maudling. Few knew it at the time, but he was gradually realizing that major police inquiries into the business affairs of the Yorkshire architect John Poulson could force his resignation – which it did just a few days later. A senior member of the Opposition had already said of the Young case: 'Home Secretaries have resigned for less', and Maudling was anxious to be fully covered when the time came for a Commons explanation.

He announced the setting up of two inquiries. A review of the existing law controlling restricted patients was to be carried out at once by Sir Carl Aarvold, Recorder of London, with Sir Denis Hill, Professor of Psychiatry at the Institute of Psychiatry and Mr G. P. Newton, director of social services for Wiltshire. Their brief was to recommend any changes for which there may be urgent need. A longer-term fundamental review of the criminal law relating to mentally abnormal offenders, and facilities for their treatment, was to be undertaken by an independent and authoritative committee under the chairmanship of Lord Butler of Saffron Walden, the distinguished former Tory politician, then Master of Trinity College, Cambridge.

Maudling had in fact telephoned Butler only a few days before, giving him brief details of his assignment; but Butler had immediately agreed to chair the committee. Maudling also told the Commons that he had 'already introduced a number of changes aimed at strengthening still further the safeguards for the protection of the public'. What he had actually done was to send out an order that no restricted patient should be discharged from any State hospital until the responsible medical officer had obtained a psychiatrist's endorsement of his fitness. Secondly, he had issued a memorandum giving psychiatric social workers and probation officers clearance to tell prospective employers the full backgrounds of discharged offenders. The two moves constituted an admission that Dr Udwin's part in Young's release had been dangerously autonomous, and that the Hadland's poisonings could have been avoided by fuller liaison with the authorities.

Maudling had a comparatively easy ride in the Commons. The Shadow Home Secretary, Mrs

Shirley Williams, recognized that 'it is impossible to be certain that there will never be any mistakes' – an unstated reference to her own years at the Home Office during the Labour Government, supervising the very department which dealt with Broadmoor releases. Mrs Williams had discussed the case with Maudling on two occasions prior to the trial, and it was her first approach that had brought the full facts of the case to his attention. Her main concern in the Commons was to ensure that the Aarvold inquiry would be able to publish a full account of the mistakes made in the Young case; Maudling made no response to this, and these facts were not made public when the Aarvold report appeared the following January. They were not even to interview such crucial figures as those members of the Hemel Hempstead probation service whose proper professional discretion gave the poisoner such a clear hand both at home and at work.

Enoch Powell raised cheers from both sides of the House when he praised the 'wonderful and devoted' work done at Broadmoor, and urged measures to maintain staff morale. No mention was made of any measures to improve the chronic understaffing at the hospital, which Mrs Williams had complained of. 'On strengthening staff, Sir Keith Joseph has done what he thinks right,' said Maudling.

Few realized the significance of the questions put by Elystan Morgan, Labour MP for Cardiganshire: 'Was the usual practice followed in this case of acting only on unanimous advice? Has the opinion of a witness at the 1962 trial that there was a continuing risk been brought to the attention of the Minister? Has not the time come for psychopathy to be treated as a condition out of the ordinary run?'

Mr Morgan had been briefed by one of his constituents, Dr Christopher Fysh, who had told Mr Justice Melford Stevenson in 1962 that Young's poisoning activities were 'extremely likely' to be repeated if he were given sufficient opportunity, and that Young's condition would never improve. Throughout the 1972 Young case, Dr Fysh – by now retired from his work at Ashford remand centre – had been sworn to silence by the Official Secrets Act, and so was able to say only privately that Young's release was bound to lead to more poisonings and more murders. It had been a 'very harrowing time' for Dr Fysh.

There followed some criticism of the long-term inquiry being chaired by a former Home Secretary, before Maudling again made promises which he was never to fulfil: 'The whole circumstances should be made public and they will be made public. We have nothing to conceal and nothing we want to conceal. We have made an exhaustive inquiry into this.'

The papers were full of the case next morning, but a discreet word in the ears of a few editors again earned Maudling more sympathy than blame. The popular press went hardest for the Government and its agents, the *Daily Mail* describing the verdict as 'an indictment of the Home Secretary, who signed the release papers; the police, for not keeping track of Young's movements; the after-care service, for not checking up on him; the Department of Health, for making it all too easy for him to buy poison; and Broadmoor itself, for allowing Young to hoodwink them that he was cured.' The *Daily Express* was not above a sick joke from Osbert Lancaster; one Florentine to another, both hiding knives behind their backs: 'Heard the latest? The Borgias have been put on probation.'

The distinction continued in the Sunday press, with the *News of the World* serializing Winifred Young's story under the heading YOUR FRIENDLY NEIGHBOURHOOD FRANKENSTEIN and the *Sunday Mirror* buying up his father's story MY SON THE POISONER. The quality press was again more circumspect, with the *Sunday Times* quoting an apposite luncheon gobbet from Maudling: 'At lunch around the beginning of last August, a guest of Reginald Maudling's asked the Home Secretary what his greatest worry was. The answer, he expected, would be Ulster. Instead, brooding for a moment, Maudling replied: "I'll tell you the thing that haunts me. It's the dilemma of Broadmoor. What do you do with people whom the doctors say are safe to let out, but who have a violent record? Do you keep them in, destroy them? Or do you take the experts' word, and accept a possible risk to society?"' It was, as *Insight* said, 'remarkable prescience'.

Restrained press coverage did much to subdue public alarm, as did an immediate check on all 331 people released from Broadmoor in the previous twelve years – which revealed nothing untoward. But the case was seized on by Tory commentators and backbenchers, predictably enough, as an example of the need for sterner treatment. Their most vociferous spokesmen were Angus Maude MP in the *Sunday Express* and Peregrine Worsthorne in the *Sunday Telegraph*. Said Maude: 'The fact is that liberal policies have not worked. Their advocates say that more time is needed to prove that they have failed – but more time is just what, at the moment, we cannot afford. Would not the best possible test be to reverse them for a period and watch the results? This would certainly reassure an anxious public – and it seems to me inconceivable that it could make things any worse.' Said Worsthorne: 'What has to be recognized is that there is a peculiar inhumanity attaching to the liberal instinct, different from but in no way less lethal than the inhumanity attaching to the reactionary instinct. The new experts who released Young were just as callous as the old experts who would not have released Young. The result of their contemporary prejudices are no less bloodthirsty than the result of the archaic prejudices which they have superseded.'

The *New Statesman*, describing Maude and Worsthorne's judgements as 'dishonest and despicable', struck the balance to which the thinking press had been aspiring: '(Young) is the kind of dangerous social misfit who, fortunately for all of us, turns up only perhaps once or twice in a century. We can probably recognize some dim reflection of ourselves in the descriptions of most of the men and women whose personalities are ruthlessly dissected in a court of law; but the actions and attitudes of Graham

Young are of a quality totally foreign to our experience.' As the *Sunday Times* more specifically put it: 'The Young affair is probably best seen as one of those cases where, in a humane system, everything that could go wrong did so.'

After a week and more of furious discussion, the case lingered in the public mind more for its implications than its own character. A string of curious after-effects began immediately with the discovery at the Sandwich, Kent, laboratories of Pfizer Ltd, a large international drugs firm, of chemicals in a sugar jar used to sweeten workers' tea. CID men launched a search for the 'copycat poisoner', announcing that staff suspected the attempted crime to have been inspired by Young's much publicized techniques. No-one drank the tea; a girl secretary noticed discolouring and raised the alarm in time; and no culprit was ever detected.

Several months later, the two firms of chemists where Young had bought his poisons – Freeman Grieve of St Albans and John Bell and Croyden of Wigmore Street, London – were both fined for failing to comply with the Pharmacy and Poisons Act of 1933, which provided controls for the sale of poison. The St Albans firm was subsequently censured by the Pharmaceutical Society.

A less savoury row erupted in April 1973 when the Criminal Injuries Compensation Board announced the sums they were paying to Young's victims. For Bob Egle's widow: £1,535. 'No amount of compensation will make up for the loss of my husband,' she said. Nevertheless, spurred on by her family, she complained at the inadequacy of the amount, and was told that she was also entitled to industrial injuries benefit – at the princely rate of 2p a week. Attempted murder victim Jethro Batt was awarded £700 plus £250 loss of earnings to compensate for acute pain, loss of hair, hallucinations, temporary insanity and after-effects which would always remain with him. The other attempted murder victim, David Tilson, was awarded £460; he had suffered the same symptoms as Batt, but understood he received less compensation because temporary impotence 'is in the eyes of the law not so important to a bachelor'. Mr Tilson's reported complaint that 'I was going around with several girls at the time and I became useless in bed' scarcely comes within the Board's criteria for assessment of compensation, which are based on those used for common law damage. One of the less seriously affected victims, Mrs Diana Smart, was awarded £367 for sufferings which included the near break-up of her marriage – 'a pittance', she called it, 'but I accepted because I wanted to try and forget the whole thing'.

Also in April 1973 fifty-year-old Howard Gronow, of Ealing, London, killed himself in the belief that he had been poisoned by Young. Gronow had been experiencing severe chest pains for eighteen months. They had begun soon after an evening he had spent in a Hemel Hempstead pub talking to a young man obsessed with chemicals and poisons. In June 1972 Gronow had seen that young man's

picture in newspapers, and discovered he was
Graham Young, inveterate poisoner. From that day,
his illness grew worse. He told doctors he was
convinced Young had poisoned him; he was told he
had a clear case of jaundice. Later he was diagnosed
as a victim of Zieve's syndrome, a rare disease
characterized by jaundice, anaemia and cirrhosis
of the liver; it is usually the result of sustained
heavy drinking. Gronow was not convinced; and
the following April he took a massive overdose of
drugs. At the inquest in Hammersmith, Dr M. Lask
confirmed the diagnosis of Zieve's syndrome. The
coroner, Dr John Burton, recorded a verdict of
suicide as a result of illness.

Meanwhile, the Aarvold Report had appeared in
January – seven months after the committee was set
up. Maudling's promise that the facts of the Young
case would be made public was honoured more in
the breach than the observance; the case was dis-
missed in one paragraph containing four sentences,
of which the most direct was: 'From our inquiries
we are satisfied that the case was dealt with in
accordance with the procedures accepted at the time
to ensure that proper weight was given to questions
of public safety.'

That apart, the report dealt thoroughly with the
problems raised by the case, and recommended
a tightening of the system from the admission of a
restricted patient through his treatment to his event-
ual discharge. The new Home Secretary, Robert
Carr, accepted the committee's recommendations,
and the new system was to include features which

would have acted as sanguine checks and balances in the case of Young himself. Within three months of the restricted patient's admission to a special hospital, the Home Office would ask the responsible medical officer whether the patient is one who requires special care in assessment. To assist in this decision, criteria were drawn up and circulated to the specialists concerned. Once the patient had been classified as requiring special assessment, the reasons were recorded and a note of this made in the Home Office file. By specific directive, that note was never to be removed from the file. Any patient who was declared not in need of this special assessment could be reclassified at any time during his stay at the hospital, in the light of new evidence.

When a classified patient came up for discharge, or transfer to an open hospital, the request was now to be referred for a second opinion to an advisory body independent of the treating hospital. The recommendation also had to be supported by the recorded views of other professional personnel – nursing staff, occupational therapists, psychiatrists and social workers – with knowledge of, and responsibility for the patient, including his rehabilitation.

The committee also persuaded the Home Secretary to set up an advisory board to screen all admissions and discharges. In special cases, the board would be given full documentation of the case, with details of the patient's offence, his history and his response to treatment, and in the case of discharge information about plans for his resettlement in the community. The advice of the responsible medical officer and all professional personnel who had dealt with the patient was to be considered by the Board, who were given power to summon them for interview about their reports. Finally, the Board now had the power to veto any application for discharge, and an obligation to explain their reasons for doing so; they could also impose special conditions on any case whose discharge they approved.

After discharge, a patient was henceforth to go wherever possible to a National Health Service hospital or a hostel for his initial period of rehabilitation. The process of transition from here to the community at large could not be completed until all those concerned with the case at every stage had considered each report fully and declared themselves satisfied with the arrangements.

Even then, the process was to continue. It was laid down that continuing care had to be specified by consultant psychiatrists and social workers on the case, and that these recommendations were to be spelt out as specifically as possible to the rehabilitation team keeping up with the discharged patient. Informal discussion of his progress and the constant exchange of information was encouraged before decisions were reached, jointly, at each stage of his new life in the community. This guidance now included, wherever possible, liaison with the patient's family and his doctor. It was recommended that much more care should be exercised in the choice of supervising officers.

Clearly, the patient's life was being taken as far out of his own hands as possible. To counteract the harmful effects of such control, the patient was now requested as soon as the question of discharge came up to give written consent for all relevant information to be disclosed. Failure to co-operate, however, would tell against him when the Home Secretary came to make the discharge decision. Built-in safeguards to prevent the abuse of personal information now included telling the patient what material was to be passed on, and to whom, plus strict controls on the use of his dossier by anyone outside the professional team supervising his discharge.

Finally, new conditions – which were not made public – were drawn up to clarify situations which might require the patient's recall to hospital. They amounted to giving the Home Secretary of the day total power 'should a situation of danger arise'.

8

His natural bent

'I read an article on thallium poisoning when I
was in America. A lot of workers in a factory died
one after the other. Their deaths were put down
to astonishingly varied causes . . . Then there was
a woman who poisoned seven people. Diagnosis
included brain tumour, encephalitis and lobar
pneumonia. The symptoms vary a good deal, I
understand. They may start with diarrhoea
and vomiting, or there may be a stage of intoxication, again it may begin with pain in the limbs
and be put down as polyneuritis or rheumatic
fever or polio – one patient was put in an
iron lung. Sometimes there's pigmentation of the
skin.'

'You talk like a medical dictionary!'

'Naturally. I've been looking it up. But one thing
always happens sooner or later. The hair falls out.
Thallium used to be used for depilation at one
time – particularly for children with ringworm.
Then it was found to be dangerous. But it's
occasionally given internally, but with very careful dosage going by the weight of the patient. It's
mainly used nowadays for rats, I believe. It's

tasteless, soluble, and easy to buy. There's only one thing; poisoning mustn't be suspected.'

It could be an extract from Graham Young's projected novel. In fact the conversation comes from Agatha Christie's novel, *The Pale Horse*, a satanic tale of Black Magic and seemingly psychic murder. The book was published in 1961, months before fourteen-year-old Graham Young claimed to have used thallium on his stepmother with uncannily similar motives. The book was mentioned at the St Albans trial by the pathologist, Professor Hugh Molesworth-Johnson, who had consulted it as one of the few textbook descriptions of the nature and effects of thallium. Young's sister, Winifred, thought it likely he read the novel soon after its publication, though Young himself denied this. Dame Agatha Christie steadfastly refused to comment on the dilemma of potential criminals benefiting from her ingenuity; but her husband, Professor Sir Max Mallowan, said – *à propos* the Young case – that she would be 'deeply distressed' were this the truth.

Young's final tally of three known murders and eight known poisonings falls short of the thirteen murders of his ideal, Dr William Palmer. But two aspects of the Young case – his own unique character and the mistakes of many in authority over him – have earned him as immortal a place in the annals of criminal notoriety. No era of British crime has matched the intrigues of Victorian suburbia for sheer relish, and the eerie glamour attached to many murderers has evaporated with the abolition of capital punishment. A humanitarian Nemesis has returned murder to its properly sordid, appalling place. In many cases, notoriety attaches to a name for reasons quite other than the nature of the crime – the question of miscarried justice, as with Evans and Hanratty, or of advances in detection methods, as with Crippen. The cases where notoriety belongs to consummately evil men, like Christie, are rare. Young's is one such case, though the charge of malevolence must be tempered with an understanding of psychopathy. Young's notoriety, furthermore, has been earned as much by flaws in a system aspiring to decent morality as by his own personality and the macabre panache of his crimes. These two questions have been fully dealt with in earlier chapters of this book; it remains only to draw attention to wider failings in the British system of crime detection, which almost conspired to leave Young at liberty, free to continue going about his business.

In 1960 Dr John Havard, of the British Medical Association, contributed a report on *The Detection of Secret Homicide* to the series of Cambridge Studies in Criminology (vol XI, 1960). In an introductory summary of his conclusions, he wrote: 'In practice, a substantial proportion of cases of homicide are accompanied by an attempt to get the death certified and registered and to get the body disposed of through the normal channels as a natural death.' Dr Havard's findings were quoted in a BMA report in 1964 on *Deaths in the Community*, which concluded that: 'the issue of a death certificate from "natural causes" is a fairly common finding in cases which are afterwards found to have been cases of homicide.' Elsewhere in the 1960 report, Dr Havard wrote: 'Several cases of death from thallium poisoning must have been disposed of as deaths from polyneuritis. Cases have increased alarmingly.'[1]

The Brodrick Report on Death Certification and Coroners, published after six and a half years' work in November 1971, made short shrift of Dr Havard's thesis and the BMA report, concluding that 'the statutory machinery has not permitted the concealment of unnatural death to any significant extent'. The report's recommendations for revising the system of death certification, and the circumstances in which post-mortems are held, are far from radical. It goes so far as to recommend a relaxation of the strict rules controlling examination before cremation.

Two of Young's three murder victims – his stepmother in 1962 and Bob Egle in 1971 – were

[1]In his last statement, Dr Havard was referring to deaths other than homicide, such as accidental or industrial poisoning, and not necessarily referring to Britain when saying 'Cases have increased alarmingly'. Young remains the first known person to have murdered by thallium poisoning in this country. It is interesting to note that a KGB agent who defected to West Germany in 1957 became seriously ill in mysterious circumstances. Tests showed that his condition was hopeless and that he was dying, but his life was just saved by the intensive effort of a team of American doctors. The illness was later diagnosed as poisoning by thallium which had been subjected to intense atomic radiation. He had been placed on the KGB 'death-list' as a traitor to Russia.

cremated after being certified dead from natural causes. The third, Fred Biggs, would also have been certified and buried as dead from natural causes – polyneuritis – had not Young's arrogance during Dr Anderson's visit to Hadland's aroused suspicion.

Young himself, at the age of fourteen, urged the cremation of his stepmother – and had his way. He attended the ceremony, as he did in Egle's case, and watched all evidence of what he claimed was his murder destroyed by fire. It was, and in effect remains, the perfect crime; he was never convicted of it in a court of law. Circumstantial evidence and the certainty of police and his family quash any doubts about the eagerness of his own subsequent confession.

When Young watched the evidence of Egle's murder similarly destroyed by fire nine years later, he was convinced he had committed the perfect crime. Only advances in forensic science in those nine years made it possible for evidence subsequently to be brought against him. But it was due to his persistence in murderous acts, and again to his own arrogant brinkmanship, that the crime was discovered at all. Young had only himself to blame that he was the recipient of the first murder charge in criminal history to follow the exhumation of cremated ashes. The forces of official detection could take no credit.

Finally, when the post-mortem on Fred Biggs was conducted by Professor Molesworth-Johnson, no trace of thallium could be found – even though the pathologist had specifically been instructed to look for it. Only chemical analysis of the organs revealed traces. Had Young not by this time given himself away, Biggs's death would also have been certified as due to natural causes.

The shortcomings of the death certification system are clearly inadequately dealt with in the Brodrick Report. But it remains equally clear that those shortcomings are in part due to the pervasive ignorance of the British medical profession about poisons.

Dr Havard dealt with both these issues in 1960. He showed the inadequacy of a law which makes no requirement for a doctor to view a body before signing the death certificate. He urged wider training of doctors in forensic science.

The Brodrick Report agreed that it would be safer for bodies to be 'viewed' before the signing of the death certificate, but found no need for close examination. It concluded that forensic medicine was of sufficient importance to merit a place in the syllabus of only four or five medical schools in the country.

Professor Francis Camps, the distinguished Home Office pathologist, who died shortly after the end of Young's second trial, seized on the case as proof of a cause to which he had devoted much of his life's work. In a speech at a forensic conference at Porton Down shortly before his death, Professor Camps derided the 'all too common medical view that forensic science is just bullet-holes'. He stressed the need for forensic training to be an integral part of every medical student's education. 'Until doctors are taught this subject properly, or at least include it in their continuing medical studies, unnecessary deaths will continue. This applies not only to homicide. It is equally true of accidental or industrial poisoning, which gets more and more common in these days of pollution. It is high time doctors realized their responsibilities in this area. It is much better to have a live patient than a convicted murderer.'

The GP in the Young case, Dr Anderson, thought Camps's demands unrealistic. 'During a week in a practice like mine, one hears of twenty or thirty incidents of reported sickness and diarrhoea. Would he have them all investigated as metal poisoning?' But in the witness box at Young's trial Dr Anderson admitted: 'I, as a general practitioner, do not know all that much about poison.' Young's 1971 victims were examined during their respective illnesses by a total of no less than forty-three doctors of differing status from GP to specialist. Not one diagnosed poisoning of any kind.

Not merely did Young make no secret of his interest in murder by poison, he was sufficiently intelligent to realize the inadequacies of both medical education and the system of death certification. It was ultimately his arrogance, as much a constituent of his psychopathic condition as his indifference to human life, which was his own undoing. Those around him, from people in positions of authority to his friends and notably his family, were for an unpardonably long period of time utterly deceived.

Epilogue to the 1995 Edition

'You never seem to get a good murder these days'
George Orwell, 'The Decline of the English
Murder', 1946.

In August 1990, two weeks before his forty-third
birthday, Graham Young reportedly died of a heart
attack in the maximum security wing of Parkhurst
prison on the Isle of Wight.

The scriptwriters of *The Young Poisoner's Handbook*, the 1995 film largely based on this book,
imply that Young in fact committed suicide, using
typically ingenious means to poison himself. As
celluloid speculation, it seems to me fair enough –
an appropriate brand, in its macabre way, of poetic
justice.

Those who ever had anything to do with Graham
Young, myself included, spent every day of every
year after his final imprisonment in permanent
expectation of reading one morning that he had died
by 'falling . . .' (in the old lags' cliché) '. . . down
the prison stairs'. Twenty years after his imprisonment I had picked up a discarded copy of *The
Times*, aboard an internal flight in the United States,

to find myself reading of Young's premature demise (hid- den away in a 'News in Brief' paragraph) without a trace of surprise.

Who in his right mind, after all, would want to spend an indefinite period incarcerated with a man who could extract poison from a stone – or in this case, perhaps, iron bars – in order to kill some time by doing just that to his everyday companions? Especially those with 'ways', as they might put it, of disposing of 'undesirables' like our Graham?

To my mind, *pace* the official Home Office version, the file remains open on Young's sudden death – apparently of natural causes – at such an early age. One day, perhaps, the Statute of Limitations will permit some ex-con to tell us the truth. In the meantime, the official line has one good thing going for it: that Young himself would have loved so abrupt and mysterious a demise. To his uniquely bizarre mind, the words 'notorious' and 'romantic' were synonymous.

During his second and last trial, in St Albans in 1972, Young gave me approving nods from the dock, even smiles, in the knowledge that I was writing this book. If I was OK by Graham – which made it distinctly easier to trust the ropey courthouse tea – it was because I was going to make him immortal. My job, as he made clear in a note passed on by his lawyers, was to make him a famous enough poisoner to merit a place in the Chamber of Horrors at Madame Tussauds.

In the event, my efforts were scarcely needed. So lavish was the newspaper coverage following his conviction – the original cuttings can be seen in the movie, plastered across the wall of his cell – that Madame T's design team must have been measuring him up even as I was still writing the original epilogue, a trainee reporter on the local paper landed with the biggest story of his young career.

A few years later, both our lives having moved on, I inadvertently discovered that Graham's dream had come true. Reluctantly yielding to the insistence of my three young sons to take them to Tussauds – an institution whose appeal has always eluded me – I was disconcerted to find myself face-to-face with the familiar features glaring from the dustjacket of my first non-fiction book. So, with no move from me, Graham had made it.

Not long after, Young sent me a spooky thank-you present. First came a phone call from a man (whose name I knew from the public prints) recently released from Wormwood Scrubs. There followed, at his request, a 'secret rendezvous' in a dim Soho clip-joint, where he handed over the proverbial brown paper package. It turned out to contain a clutch of drawings – drawings to churn the stomach, with spindly matchstick men, syringes marked POISON poking from their arms, fighting for space with swastikas and other trademark Young graffiti.

'These are for you,' beamed my new friend. 'Graham wanted you to have them.' With which he snatched them straight back, proposing that we go into business together: photocopy them, number them as limited editions (signed by the artist), and make a few bob for ourselves by selling them to

189

'Graham Young fans'. It was, I think, the only time in my journalistic career that I literally 'made an excuse and left', abandoning the booty to my bemused but delighted host.

'There's more,' he cried after my fleeing shadow. 'Graham's left you some stuff in his will. Notebooks and that.' Fifteen years on, reading of Young's death over an in-flight cup of American tea, I fell to wondering what the Royal Mail might have in store for me on my return home. Nothing, in the event, materialized – to my redoubled relief when I learned from Brian Masters, biographer of Dennis Nilsen, that he had inherited the saucepans in which the 'Cricklewood Monster' had boiled his victims' dismembered corpses. Such legacies, apparently, are regarded in the trade as an all but obligatory gesture from these master-criminal Johnsons to their Boswells.

By this time my book had earned me the acquaintance of Lord Longford, whose tireless work on behalf of redeemable criminals is well-known – if unfairly rewarded, to this day, with heartless and lazy satire. Whatever the merits of his case for the release of those widely thought beyond the pale, such as the 'Moors murderess' Myra Hindley, Longford has proved a noble pioneer in the rehabilitation of the mentally ill offender – the momentary lawbreaker who ultimately deserves another chance in the society which drove him or her off the rails in the first place.

Graham Young, to my mind, was never one such. But it was the best instincts of a decent system which had released him, however disastrous the consequences, as my book had attempted to make clear. With the encouragement of Longford and his colleague Peter Thompson, himself a former Broadmoor patient, I became an active member of the Matthew Trust, a group working towards a better understanding of the problems of mentally ill offenders (and their victims) in the context of their return to the world at large. The occasional tragedy following such releases was far out-numbered by (and, of course, far more publicised than) the cast-histories of those who returned, as invisibly as possible, to lead decent, productive and happier lives. But the problem of those 'released to kill again' remained, as did the cruel pressures on families expected to care for seriously ill rela-tives.

At the public meetings of the Matthew Trust I often found myself approached by interested parties, from psychiatrists to prison visitors, in regular con-tact with Graham Young. There was scope for much black humour as they told me: 'Graham's asked me to tell you he'd love to see you. You really ought to pay him a visit. Let him make you a cup of tea . . .' It was sincerely said, by well-meaning people, but I could never quite summon the *sang-froid* to take Young up on his invitation.

More than two decades on – for all the efforts of organizations like the Matthew Trust, and the reforms following Lord Butler's report on the Young case, implemented in the 1983 Mental Health Act – little seems to have changed. In April 1994

Broadmoor was reported to be 'at boiling-point', with staff 'seething' over management proposals to reduce the hospital's 'penitential' atmosphere – specifically, a new 'non-seclusion' policy allowing patients more freedom of movement within the intimidating Gothic building and its grounds.

The management's intentions, to 'treat patients as human beings' and avoid institutionalizing them, were as sound as the staff's objections. Already that year there had been ninety attacks (double the previous year's figures) by patients on staff – who were condemned by the mental health charity MIND for considering industrial action. 'Rather than defusing volatile situations,' said MIND's policy director, Liz Sayce, 'the use of seclusion simply stokes up future problems.'

'It's all very well to say that, sitting some distance away,' replied Frank Mone, the Prison Officers Association's branch chairman. 'They are not here getting attacked by patients. The "open" regime [recently] instituted here has given patients more rights than those looking after them.' At least thirty per cent of the attacks, he went on, were 'a direct result' of the non-seclusion policy.

'At the time of their apprehension all these people were headline news – uncontrollable, violent and dangerous in a way that could turn your stomach,' said another POA official, Brian Caton. While Broadmoor's management defended its proposals as 'morally right and humane', the staff condemned them as 'revolutionary and dangerous'.

In the wake of the controversy, in July 1994, a

Department of Health working group recommended that Britain's three top-security 'special hospitals' – Broadmoor, Rampton and Ashworth – be drastically reduced in size, and patients dispersed to new, custom-built units housing a maximum of two hundred each.

At the time of writing, the three hospitals accommodate a total of more than 1,500 patients, with Broadmoor (in Berkshire) and Rampton (in Nottinghamshire) housing around 500 each, and Ashworth (on Merseyside) almost 600. Nothing has been done about the 1994 proposals – already a year old when they were published – which would require the construction of at least four new high-security hospitals around the country. It was thought extremely unlikely that the government would take any action before the next general election, because of the 'Nimby' ['Not in my back yard'] factor as much as the cost. 'Finding suitable sites, acceptable to the local population,' according to Whitehall, 'could take years.'

With the Conservative government's *penchant* for closing more hospitals than they open, and for saving money by releasing mental patients into the care of their families, there seem likely in the meantime to be many more such tragedies as that of Georgina Robinson, a twenty-seven-year-old occupational therapist at the Edith Morgan Centre, Torquay, who was savagely stabbed to death by a paranoid schizophrenic, Andrew Robinson [no relation], in September 1993.

South African-born, Robinson had been sent to

Broadmoor in 1978, at the age of twenty-one, for the attempted murder of a girlfriend who had rejected him. The Broadmoor psychiatrist who diagnosed schizophrenia 'strongly' recommended a restriction order 'without limit of time', as 'his illness and potential dangerousness are likely to last a long time.' Within three years, nonetheless, Andrew Robinson was released from Broadmoor to a less secure psychiatric hospital, and nine months later given a conditional discharge by the Home Secretary of the day, William Whitelaw.

In and out of psychiatric hospitals over the next twelve years, with his family frantically urging medication, he wound up at the Edith Morgan Centre, where he told staff that he needed to kill someone 'to win respect'. Allowed to leave the Centre without the permission of his responsible medical officer (contrary to Section 3 of the 1983 Mental Health Act), he bought a kitchen knife in Torquay on 25 August 1993 and travelled to London intent on killing the Prime Minister. Finding parliament in recess, he returned to Torquay. 'He seems very calm after his trip to London,' noted a nurse who examined him. An hour later he brutally attacked and killed Georgina Robinson, a highly promising young therapist who was soon to have been married. 'I'm sorry it was her,' he said as he was led away. 'I meant it for [one of the doctors].' To another nurse he said: 'It should have been John Major.'

Readers of the Graham Young story may well find that of Andrew Robinson all too familiar.

Mistakes were made at many levels, concluded the subsequent inquiry chaired by Sir Louis Blom-Cooper: by the unit from which Robinson walked out to buy the knife; by social service and psychiatric staff who 'failed to recognize they had more power to recall Robinson than they realized'; by a system which failed to ensure that his records contained full details of the earlier attack (which had seen him first confined to Broadmoor); and by ministers who 'still fail to recognize', in the words of the *Guardian*, 'that the 1983 Mental Health Act was devised for a different era and must be replaced.'

To Sir Louis, the failings of the system were prompted by 'a fundamentally flawed statutory framework.' To Georgina Robinson's mother, Wendy, 'Closing the mental institutions and putting patients in the community was a cheap option, but it has turned out to be more expensive than they thought. Innocent victims like Georgina have paid the price. She paid with her life.'

'You never seem to get a good murder these days,' wrote George Orwell in 1946, complaining on behalf of the well-fed, piped-and-slippered Englishman settling down to his post-prandial, Sunday afternoon *News of the World*. The wartime Cleft Chin Murder, an account of which he was reviewing for *Tribune*, disappointed Orwell by its 'pitiful and sordid' character, 'interesting only from a sociological and perhaps a legal point of view.' Where were the middle-class suburban poisoners of yesteryear, where the outwardly respectable little professional men, led astray by clandestine lust and forced to murder in the name of propriety? Where were murderers of the calibre of Joseph Smith, who played 'Nearer, My God, to Thee' on the harmonium while his wife was drowning in the next room?

The peculiarly British fascination for the gruesome detail of cases like Young's should not overlook the faults (and the strengths) of the system which allowed him to resume his criminal career. At every stage of his murderous progress Young understood that system and turned its weaknesses to his own benefit. Yet this book is not to be read as an indictment of liberalism; quite the reverse. When the truth became public about Young's premature release from Broadmoor, and the second round of poisonings it had permitted, the Home Office inevitably called his case 'unique', surmising that 'people like him slip through the net only once in a century'. And perhaps, apart from the arbitrary time-scale, they were right. Right-wing critics seized the hour to attack the weakness of our methods of dealing with mentally disturbed offenders. But what they would term weaknesses when discussing a historic case like Young's are otherwise the system's very strengths.

The case quite rightly provoked a major review of that system. But Young's story, apart from the fascination of his own character, remains primarily one of human failings. As I concluded in the prologue to the first edition of this book, published in 1974: 'It can be argued that those failings cost lives, but it should not be forgotten that the human qualities which engendered them have saved many more.'

The problems raised for civilized society by a Graham Young will remain timeless, and must be a matter for the individual conscience to set against whatever system prevails. The real indictment of the present system, twenty years on, is that so little has been done to stop it happening all over again.

Anthony Holden
London, 1995.

Acknowledgements

Much of the original research that led to this book was shared by myself with three other reporters then working on the *Evening Echo*, Hemel Hempstead – John Marquis, Philip Smith and Lee Harrison. Much credit for that project was also due to the paper's deputy editor, David Francis, who supervised it, and to the editor, Ivor Lewis, forgiving two of us almost six clear months on the one story – an unusual enterprise on a provincial paper.

Some of the material in chapter five originally appeared in the form of an article for the *New Statesman* – to whose editor, Anthony Howard, I am grateful for permission to re-use it.

I would also like to thank Alan Gordon Walker and Hilary Rubinstein for unflagging help and advice when the book encountered some unexpected hurdles. The 1995 reissue owes everything to Bill Scott-Kerr of Transworld, and Mass/Sam Taylor Productions, makers of the stylish movie *The Young Poisoner's Handbook*.

Dr Francis Camps, the distinguished Home Office pathologist, was helping me with characteristically intense enthusiasm until his sudden death soon after Young's 1972 trial. His contribution to the book would have made it a better one; but in acknowledgement of what there is of him in it, and in tribute to his work in the field of forensic science, I respectfully dedicate it to his memory.

Index

205

A SELECTION OF
RELATED TITLES AVAILABLE FROM
CORGI BOOKS AND BANTAM PRESS

14248	2	**LIVE FROM THE BATTLEFIELD**	Peter Arnett	£6.99
13818	5	**INSIDE THE BRITISH ARMY**	Antony Beevor	£6.99
13337	X	**THE PROVISIONAL IRA**		
			Patrick Bishop & Eamonn Mallie	£5.99
13679	4	**REBELS**	Peter de Rosa	£6.99
13582	8	**THE GOD SQUAD**	Paddy Doyle	£5.99
03831	2	**BIG DEAL**	Anthony Holden	£7.99
02472	9	**THE TARNISHED CROWN** (Hardback)		
			Anthony Holden	£16.99
02468	0	**TCHAIKOVSKY** (Hardback)	Anthony Holden	£17.99
14259	X	**THE FBI**	Ronald Kessler	£6.99
13892	4	**FIFTY YEARS IN THE SYSTEM**	Jimmy Laing	£5.99
13727	8	**THE VIEW FROM NO. 11**	Nigel Lawson	£9.99
13953	X	**SOME OTHER RAINBOW**		
			John McCarthy & Jill Morrell	£5.99
14127	5	**BRAVO TWO ZERO**	Andy McNab	£5.99
13946	7	**NICOLA**	Nicola Owen	£4.99
13311	6	**MOSSAD**	Ronald Payne	£4.99
99533	9	**GROTESQUE LIBELS**	Adam Raphael	£5.99
03779	0	**THE AUTOBIOGRAPHY OF A THIEF** (Hardback)		
			Bruce Reynolds	£15.99
13058	3	**THE MARILYN CONSPIRACY**	Milo Speriglio	£3.99
14204	2	**OFFICIAL AND CONFIDENTIAL**	Anthony Summers	£6.99
99512	6	**NOBODY NOWHERE**	Donna Williams	£6.99
14198	4	**SOMEBODY SOMEWHERE**	Donna Williams	£5.99
12858	9	**JACK THE RIPPER**	Colin Wilson & Robin Odell	£5.99
13452	X	**THE DAY THE LAUGHTER STOPPED**	David Yallop	£6.99
13288	8	**IN GOD'S NAME**	David Yallop	£6.99
13454	6	**DELIVER US FROM EVIL**	David Yallop	£5.99
12763	9	**TO THE ENDS OF THE EARTH**	David Yallop	£6.99
13453	8	**BEYOND REASONABLE DOUBT?**	David Yallop	£6.99